THE
HISTORICAL
BOOKS

GENERAL EDITORS

Gene M. Tucker, *Old Testament*

Charles B. Cousar, *New Testament*

INTERPRETING
I · B · T
BIBLICAL TEXTS

THE
HISTORICAL
BOOKS

Richard D. Nelson

ABINGDON PRESS
Nashville

THE HISTORICAL BOOKS

Copyright © 1998 by Abingdon Press

This book is printed on elemental-chlorine-free paper.

Library of Congress Cataloging-in-Publication Data

Nelson, Richard D. (Richard Donald), 1945–
  The historical books / Richard D. Nelson.
    p.   cm.
  Includes bibliographical references and index.
  ISBN 0-687-00843-3 (pbk. : alk. paper)
    1. Bible.   O.T.   Historical Books—Introductions.   2. Bible. O.T. Historical books—Criticism, interpretation, etc.   I. Title.
  BS1205.2.N45 1998
  222'.061—dc21   98-28160
                                                              CIP

Scripture quotations, except where indicated, are from the New Revised Standard Version Bible, copyright © 1989, by the Division of Christian Education of the National Council of the Churches of Christ in the United States of America. Used by permission.

Quotations noted KJV are from the King James or Authorized Version of the Bible.

Other quotations are the author's translation.

05 06 07—10 9 8 7 6

MANUFACTURED IN THE UNITED STATES OF AMERICA

CONTENTS

FOREWORD

Biblical texts create worlds of meaning, and invite readers to enter them. When readers enter such textual worlds, which are often strange and complex, they are confronted with theological claims. With this in mind, the purpose of this series is to help serious readers in their experience of reading and interpreting, to provide guides for their journeys into textual worlds. The controlling perspective is expressed in the operative word of the title—*interpreting*. The primary focus of the series is not so much on the world *behind* the texts or out of which the texts have arisen (though these worlds are not irrelevant) as on the world *created by* the texts in their engagement with readers.

Each volume addresses two questions. First, What are the critical issues of interpretation that have emerged in the recent history of scholarship and to which serious readers of the texts need to be sensitive? Some of the concerns of scholars are interesting and significant, but frankly peripheral to the interpretative task. Others are more central. How they are addressed influences decisions readers make in the process of interpretation. Thus the authors call attention to these basic issues and indicate their significance for interpretation.

Second, in struggling with particular passages or sections of material, How can readers be kept aware of the larger world related by the text as a whole? How can they both see the forest and examine individual trees? How can students encountering the story of David and Bathsheba in 2 Samuel 11 read it in light of its context in the larger story, the Deuteronomistic History that includes the books of Deuteronomy through 2 Kings? How can readers of Galatians fit what they learn into the theological coherence and polarities of the larger perspective drawn from all the letters of Paul? Thus each volume provides an overview of the literature as a whole.

The aim of the series is clearly pedagogical. The authors offer their own understanding of the issues and texts, but are more concerned about guiding the reader than engaging in debates with other scholars. The series is meant to serve as a resource, alongside other resources such as commentaries and specialized studies, to aid students in the exciting and often risky venture of interpreting biblical texts.

Gene M. Tucker
General Editor, Old Testament

Charles B. Cousar
General Editor, New Testament

PREFACE

This volume is designed to introduce students to the historical books of the Old Testament. I have directed it primarily at those who are just beginning their work with biblical texts. For this reason, little is taken for granted about what the reader may know about the art and science of biblical interpretation. Through this book, however, I also hope to offer guidance for more seasoned interpreters who may wish to rethink and revitalize the way they read the Bible. I have tried to produce a sort of road map through the interpretative complexities of the historical books. I have sought to provide the basic knowledge and background needed to be a self-reliant reader and interpreter of the books Joshua through Nehemiah. This work cannot replace standard exegetical resources such as commentaries and critical introductions. Instead, it is intended to be a resource for their effective use.

The primary focus of this series is not the historical world behind texts or out of which they grew, but the worlds created in the here and now when an alert and knowledgeable interpreter reads them. Given that these are *historical* books, however, the reader obviously must pay attention to history. Knowledge about Israel's past and the history of the composition of these books is vital to energize and facilitate the task of interpretation. Yet looking at the past should not divert the interpreter from the primary goal of reading for the present.

Part 1 (chapters 1–3) deals with relevant issues that emerge from the task of reading these books. It introduces the concepts of history, history writing, and narrative. It offers a simple framework of events and periods that can be used to locate the incidents reported in the historical books or presupposed by them. Part 1 also explains various standard interpretative methods. These are applied to a sample text in order to show how they can be used to uncover meaning. Beginning interpreters are urged to get their feet wet and their hands dirty by working on 2 Samuel 24.

Part 2 (chapters 4–10) is a guided tour of each historical book in its final canonical form. These descriptions pay attention to earlier works embedded in the present books, to matters of organization and structure, to literary plot, and to the succession of audiences to whom these books have spoken. These chapters ought to be read with one's Bible open. They are intended to engage the reader in an active process of interaction with the biblical texts.

The ultimate goal of this interpretative process is to hear the claims made by the Old Testament historical books on the reader, on the reader's faith community, and on the world. These books make claims about who God is, what God does, and what God stands for. They seek to shape the identity, faith, and behavior of those who read them. This volume intends to help the interpreter hear those claims and make sense out of them.

"To teach is to learn twice" (Joseph Joubert, *Pensées*). I am particularly grateful to those Gettysburg Seminary students who have participated in my first semester required course, "The Pentateuch and Historical Books," over the last sixteen years. They have served as guinea pigs for much of the content and methodology of this book.

OUTLINES OF THE HISTORICAL BOOKS

THE BOOK OF JOSHUA

1:1–12:24	— Joshua conquers the land
13:1–21:45	— Joshua divides the land
22:1–24:33	— Warnings about the future

THE BOOK OF JUDGES

1:1–2:5	— Unfinished conquest
2:6–12:15	— A succession of judges
13:1–16:31	— Samson the lone hero
17:1–21:25	— Disorder and infidelity

THE BOOKS OF 1 AND 2 SAMUEL

1 Sam 1:1–8:22	— The story of Samuel
1 Sam 9:1–15:35	— The story of Samuel and Saul
1 Sam 16:1–2 Sam 1:27	— The story of Saul and David
2 Sam 2:1–8:18	— David under the blessing
2 Sam 9:1–24:25	— David under the curse

THE BOOKS OF 1 AND 2 KINGS

1 Kgs 1:1–11:43	— Solomon in glory and dishonor
1 Kgs 12:1–16:34	— The effect of folly and sin
1 Kgs 17:1–2 Kgs 8:29	— Israel and the prophets

2 Kgs 9:1–12:21   — Revolution and reform
2 Kgs 13:1–17:41   — Israel slides into disaster
2 Kgs 18:1–23:30   — Judah's disobedience and reform
2 Kgs 23:31–25:30   — Destruction and exile

THE BOOKS OF 1 AND 2 CHRONICLES

1 Chr 1:1–9:44   — Israel's family tree
1 Chr 10:1–29:30   — David and the temple
2 Chr 1:1–9:31   — Solomon and the temple
2 Chr 10:1–36:23   — Kings of the temple community

THE BOOKS OF EZRA AND NEHEMIAH

Ezra 1:1–6:22   — Rebuilding the temple
Ezra 7:1–10:44   — Reforming the community
Neh 1:1–7:73   — Rebuilding the city wall
Neh 8:1–10:39   — Hearing and doing the law
Neh 11:1–13:31   — Further reforms by Nehemiah

PART ONE

ISSUES
IN
READING
THE
HISTORICAL
BOOKS

CHAPTER 1

WHAT ARE WE READING?

WHAT ARE THE HISTORICAL BOOKS?

The classification "historical books" was used by the church fathers (for example, Cyril of Jerusalem, d. 386) to refer to Genesis through Esther. However, in common scholarly usage this designation usually encompasses Joshua, Judges, Samuel, Kings, Chronicles, Ezra, and Nehemiah.[1] Ruth and Esther (along with apocryphal books like Judith or 1 and 2 Maccabees) are also arguably historical books, but are not covered in this volume. The historical books fall naturally into two divisions, based on their place in the history of the canon, their time of origin, and their thematic interests.

The earlier of these two historical complexes consists of the books of Joshua, Judges, Samuel, and Kings. Jewish tradition groups these books together to make up a portion of the canon called the Former Prophets.[2] Taken together, these books tell the story of Israel's history in the land. This story begins with the invasion of Canaan (the first chapters of Joshua) and ends with the exile of the people of Judah from their land (the last chapters of 2 Kings). Scholars usually call this lengthy piece of history writing the Deuteronomistic History (abbreviated DH) because of its close conceptual connections to Deuteronomy (see chapter 4). DH presents Israel's story in relation to the question of obedience or disobedience to the "book of the law," that is, the book of Deuteronomy. This law book is mentioned for the first time in Joshua 1:8 and for the last time in 2 Kings 23:24-25. The Deuteronomistic History looks backward in time, seeking to explain the successes and failures of the nation in terms of its observance or violation of God's law.

The second large historical complex consists of the books of Chronicles and Ezra-Nehemiah.[3] In the Hebrew Bible, these books appear at the end of the third division of the canon called the Writings. In defiance of their chronological order, Ezra-Nehemiah usually comes before Chronicles in Jewish canonical tradition. However in some Hebrew manuscripts, including the very early Aleppo Codex (tenth century CE), Chronicles opens the Writings section and Ezra-Nehemiah closes it. In the Christian canonical tradition, derived from the Greek Old Testament, these books follow Kings. The Christian arrangement thus follows the principle of chronological order.

The present form of Chronicles is linked to Ezra and Nehemiah as a continuous story by the overlap of 2 Chronicles 36:22-23 and Ezra 1:1-3. However, scholars continue to debate whether this second historical complex ever made up a single unified work in the same sense that the Deuteronomistic History did. Those who emphasize the similarities in style and outlook between Chronicles and Ezra-Nehemiah sometimes designate them as the Chronistic Work or the Chronicler's History. More recently, it has become common to point to indications that the two works developed separately as independent literary compositions. Because Chronicles and Ezra-Nehemiah address similar audiences and share a similar theological perspective, I have chosen to use a more neutral designation and call them the Chronistic books.

Both the Deuteronomistic History and the Chronistic books were constructed on the basis of earlier written sources. Some of these sources were literary works of a historical nature. For example, Judges 9 (Abimelech's monarchy) and 2 Kings 9:1–10:27 (Jehu's revolt) are small, self-contained narratives with a historical concern. Five of the clearest instances of these earlier history-rylike compositions are:

• An earlier book of Joshua (Joshua 2–11) that tells of a unified conquest of Canaan. It uses the fearful reaction of Israel's enemies and the figure of Joshua to organize individual conquest stories (see chapter 5).
• The Ark Story (roughly 1 Samuel 4–6 and 2 Samuel 6) describes the itinerary and "adventures" of the ark of the covenant from its battlefield capture by the Philistines to its installation by David in Jerusalem (see chapter 7).
• The Rise of David (roughly 1 Samuel 16–2 Samuel 5). This is a coordinated collection of narratives about David and Saul. The interpretative notes and comments that bind these accounts together affirm that the Lord had effectively given the kingship over to David even during Saul's lifetime (see chapter 7).
• The Throne Succession Story (approximately 2 Samuel 9–20 and 1 Kings 1–2). This is a single, unified narrative rather like a historical short story. It recounts the palace intrigues and family struggles that resulted in Solomon succeeding to the throne of his father, David (see chapter 7).
• The Nehemiah Memorial (Neh 1:1–7:5 and 12:31–13:31). This is a first-person report of Nehemiah's efforts as a Persian appointee to regularize the situation of postexilic Jerusalem. It calls upon God to remember Nehemiah's virtues (Neh 13:31) and seeks to provide a political justification for his activities (see chapter 10).

WHAT IS HISTORY?

"History," like art or obscenity, is easier to recognize than to define.[4] An elementary school definition might be something like "the past as it actually happened." The classic statement of this positivistic view of the historian's task is that of Leopold von Ranke (d. 1886), who asserted that history seeks to discover "how it really was" *(wie es eigentlich gewesen)*. However, most adults soon learn that history as it is actually taught and written is a much more complicated phenomenon. For one thing, the past is only selectively known and only selectively interpreted. Not all past events are available to the historian. Most happenings are not recorded or remembered, and most records disappear.

Usually only the affairs of the rich and powerful or certain urgent and critical events that influence a whole society ever enter the historical record. Thus from its very beginning in the ancient world, history's story has typically been about kings and wars. The huge mass of details concerning the daily lives of ordinary people does not become part of what is investigated as history.

It is also obvious that historians cannot recover or set forth past events in anything like an objective way. Both the sources themselves and the historians who interpret them reflect political and cultural biases. Present-day historians try to recognize the biases of historical sources and correct for them. Modern historians also usually attempt to recognize and tame their own prejudices. Yet, the unconscious prejudices of time, geography, class, and culture are still inevitably at work, even today.[5] In contrast, those who wrote history before the Renaissance rarely took a critical stance over against their sources or ever seem to have been conscious of their own biases. Lorenzo Valla's debunking of the authenticity of the so-called Donation of Constantine (1440) is often cited as the watershed case leading to the critical use of sources by historians. Medieval historians were dominated by religious ideology. Since the Renaissance, however, secular explanations for historical developments have increasingly replaced religious ones, and a historian's prejudices have tended to have more to do with nationalism or political philosophy.

The contributions of other disciplines, notably archaeology, anthropology, and economics, have revolutionized modern history. However, history remains fundamentally the product of a disciplined concern with written records. This means that trying to produce a history of a preliterate people inevitably leads to an impoverished product. Perhaps one may say something about large-scale trends and structures based on the evidence of archaeology and the insights of cultural anthropology. However, without the raw material of recorded events, names, and places, there can be no narrative, no story. Therefore, even if one may come to know a good deal about periods before the existence of written records, such times and peoples inevitably remain "prehistoric." Without a narrative of events, there can be no genuine history.

Finally, the historical enterprise requires an understanding of time and a sense of chronology that goes beyond the repeated cycle of agricultural seasons or an endlessly repetitive religious calendar. An urge to keep track of linear chronology probably developed only with the emergence of centralized state governments in the ancient world. In order to rule effectively, bureaucrats and administrators had to count passing years and record successive reigns. It is for this reason that the earliest historical accounts are the king lists, annalistic inscriptions, and chronicles that arose from the royal governments of ancient Mesopotamia and Egypt.

WHAT IS HISTORIOGRAPHY?

Historiography, like its cousin biography, is primarily a type of literature. In Western culture, at least, the classic examples of historiography as a literary form are the works of the Greek historians Herodotus and Thucydides. The word *history* comes from the Greek verb *historein*, "to narrate what has been learned by inquiry." By a happy linguistic accident, this verb is also related to the noun *histor*, "one learned in the law" and thus "a judge." These Greek words designate the two chief concerns of historiography, to narrate the past and to make judgments about it. In other words, historiography or history writing is more than just a bare catalog of past events. It is a matter of interpretation.

By its very nature historiography is an ideological and interpretative enterprise. Historians write because they have convictions about the past and present and want to communicate their beliefs. For this reason, historiography makes value judgments about events and people. Were they helpful, beneficial, moral, and noble? Or harmful, destructive, wicked, and dishonorable?

The first level of interpretation in historiography is selection. Which events and people are worth the reader's notice? Which incidents made a difference in the course of events? Which may be ignored as inconsequential? For example, the historian who wrote the book of Kings failed entirely to mention the battle of Qarqar (853 BCE), certainly one of the most important events in the career of King Ahab of Israel. Moreover, this same writer chose to portray Ahab's father, Omri, in a mere eight verses (1 Kgs 16:21-28), even though modern historians credit him with being one of Israel's most important rulers. The author of Chronicles goes even further and effectively eliminates Omri, mentioning his name only once in passing. As historiographers, these biblical writers used their own interpretative criteria for making judgments about what to select as important.

A second level of historical interpretation is organization. The tale of the past is not simply told willy-nilly. Historiography characteristically imposes some sort of structure on the past and provides links between events. The writer of history seeks to establish patterns in the incidents reported and provide a unified interpretative outlook. Authors of historiography can achieve these goals by following a chronological scheme (as in the case of Kings or Ezra-Nehemiah) or by centering on certain themes (as in Joshua or Chronicles). Historiographers can also accomplish narrative organization by tracing repeated or typical patterns. Thus, the heroes of the book of Judges are presented in a cyclical scheme easily discernible in Judges 3:7-11. After apostasy on the part of Israel, the Lord gives them over to oppression by enemy kings and peoples. When they repent and call on the Lord for help, a judge emerges as a national savior.

Another example of historiographic organization can be found in the presentation of David's rise to royal power (1 Sam 16:14– 2 Sam 5:12). Here the unifying principle of organization is Saul's decline in contrast to David's advance to royal power. "The LORD was with him [David] but had departed from Saul" (1 Sam 18:12). If one wished to illustrate this narrative pattern on a graph, Saul's career would be represented by a line that falls over time, while a second line for David rises. Each individual narrative serves as a building block to construct this overarching theme. Yet another example of an extended organizing pattern is the repeated phrase "after the death of" (Josh 1:1; Judg 1:1; 2 Sam 1:1; 2 Kgs 1:1), which unifies the present shape of the Former Prophets.

The organizing structures of ancient history writing are some-times subtle, even elusive. Events may simply be laid out one after the other without any discernible arrangement. There may be no suggestion that certain episodes are any more critical or more important than others are. There may be no interpretative summaries or organizing conclusions. This compositional style, called parataxis, was characteristic of the ancient Greek historian Herodotus. The practice of parataxis explains why biblical books sometimes seem to end abruptly on what modern readers judge to be a lame note (for example, 2 Kgs 25:27-30 or Jonah

4:11). Sometimes the use of parataxis invites the reader to discover meaningful analogies between events. In Kings, for example, analogies exist between several pairs of narratives. Examples are 1 Kings 3:16-28 and 2 Kings 6:26-31 (two mothers disputing about their children), 1 Kings 10:1-13 and 2 Kings 20:12-19 (wisdom and folly with visitors), and 2 Kings 9:30-37 and 11:13-16 (a wicked queen is killed).

A third level of interpretation typical of historiography is the drive to establish patterns of causation. What circumstances and causes brought about the events described? What later events and states of affairs did they produce in turn? Theories of historical causation have changed over the centuries. In the Romantic nineteenth century, the characters and talents of great individuals (such as Luther, Genghis Khan, or Napoleon) were understood as shaping history in a decisive way. A frequently quoted line from Thomas Carlyle expresses this perspective: "The history of the world is but the biography of great men."

Geography, climate, technology, and sociological factors play a central role in modern discussions of historical causation. Some historians have proposed organic models in which societies compete with one another and adapt to meet new challenges.[6] The notion that history is in some sense directed by a future goal toward which it is moving can be found in the writings of both Hegel and Marx. For Hegel this goal was being achieved by the workings of an idealistically conceived "universal reason." For Marx, history's inevitable goal was a classless society characterized by rational economic cooperation. Many current historians join Marx in considering economics and class struggle as history's chief causative factors.

In the ancient and medieval worlds, those who wrote history often cited supernatural or divine forces as causative explanations for events. Thus, Assyrian and Egyptian kings invoked the gods to explain their successes. In an inscription from the ninth century BCE, the king of Moab publicly credited his success in recapturing territory from Israel to his national god Chemosh: "He saved me from all the kings and caused me to triumph over all my enemies." The king also blamed earlier national reverses on the anger of Chemosh.[7] The system of historical causation found in this inscription is remarkably similar to that of the book of Joshua. For classical Greek and Roman authors, history's system of causation was primarily moral. Herodotus attributed the causes of the Persian War in part to divine retribution for unjust acts and human pride.

Supernatural causation faded in the later classical historians, but returned with a vengeance in early and medieval Christian historiography. For Eusebius (about 325), the political triumph of Christianity was the result of God's intervention (*Ecclesiastical History*, especially Book X). Divine causation remained a gradually declining feature of historiography from the Venerable Bede (*Ecclesiastical History of the English People*, 731) to Cotton Mather (*Ecclesiastical History of New England*, 1702). The rise of humanism diminished the tendency to find a role for God in history, and the Enlightenment effectively eradicated it. When the Rationalist Edward Gibbon produced *The Decline and Fall of the Roman Empire* (1776–88), he was able to describe the rise of Christianity in a fully objective manner, treating religion as one would any other social institution. In sharp contrast, biblical historiography follows the ancient practice of discovering the true causes of earthly events in the passions and purposes of the God of Israel.

THE READER AND HISTORIOGRAPHY

Philosophers of history have advanced various definitions for historiography. One factor common to most of them is the recognition that historiography explores the past in order to influence the present. Two perceptive definitions of historiography make this point:

• "An extensive, continuous, written composition based upon various materials, some originally traditional and oral, others written, and devoted to a particular subject or historical period.... Writers of history intended to document, reflect on, and organize the past in order to understand, legitimate, or define in some way the institutional and social reality of their own time."[8]
• "History is the intellectual form in which a civilization renders account to itself of its past."[9]

The writer of history is as much concerned with the contemporary audience as with past events. The Greek historian Thucydides wrote to furnish his readers with an understanding of the causes of war, not only of the recent war between Athens and Sparta, but also of similar conflicts that would inevitably occur in the future. The first-century Jewish historian Josephus *(The Jewish War)* sought to honor his imperial sponsors and safeguard his own reputation. In short, history writing is an enterprise with a contemporary purpose.

Consequently, historiography is not the same thing as objective, detached reporting. It is a type of literature, and as such, it has a literary intent. The writer of history seeks to make the past alive for the reader by telling a story. Historiography as narrative creates a world of meaning for its readers and invites them to share in this world. It recounts past events systematically, tracing cause and effect. However, it does not do this entirely out of some antiquarian or scientific interest. Instead, historiography intends to elucidate the meaning or significance of past events for an audience presupposed by its author. To put it another way, historiography seeks to explain something about the present on the basis of the past. Sometimes it seeks to provide a means for explaining and legitimating change—that is, how and why today differs from the past. Often it intends to define and strengthen the national, ethnic, or religious identity of its readers.

To interpret the historical books of the Old Testament, the reader must first seek to understand their relationship to the past as reflected in the oral and written sources they used. The employment of sources of some sort demonstrates that a writer intends to be writing history rather than some other kind of literature. Unlike the writer of fiction, the writer of history does not simply make it all up. The broad outline of what was thought to be the story of Israel's past was commonly known and publicly recited. Because ancient Israelite readers already knew much of their own story, the writers of biblical history were compelled to tell that story in a way that would be accepted. Moreover, the historian's oral and written sources would have been at least potentially available to contemporary readers. Therefore, the historian could not ignore or deform these sources out of recognizable shape. The book of Kings demonstrates this three-way interrelationship between sources, historian, and reader by citing three written sources that appear to have been accessible to its readership (1 Kgs 11:41; 14:19; 14:29).

The modern reader must also think about the relationship

between the biblical historians and their original audience. The authors or editors of the historical books intended to influence their readers in certain ways. Biblical historians sought to strengthen Israel's identity as a people specially chosen by the Lord. They endeavored to claim Israel's ancestral lands in the face of opposition (Joshua). They urged loyalty to God and sought to spur obedience to divine law (Judges). They recounted and reshaped the past in order to support and give legitimacy to institutions such as the dynasty of David (Samuel) or the ceremonies of the Jerusalem Temple (Chronicles). Therefore, the interpreter must always pay careful attention to the political, social, and cultural circumstances of the first readers. For the present reader, then, biblical historiography attests to the past with a sort of double vision. It is just as much an indicator of its own time and the situation of its original audience as it is a witness to the past story it recounts.

Biblical historiography also has a relationship to the future and future readers. Historians do not write for the immediate moment or only for a contemporary audience. History is also a word addressed to posterity. Thucydides was conscious of this when he declared that his history was "composed, not as a prize-essay to be heard for the moment, but as a possession for all time."[10] The ancient practice of erecting inscriptions or placing them into the foundations and walls of public buildings shows a similar concern for future audiences. Biblical historiography was the product of a learned, scribal tradition linked both to the past and to the future. The biblical writer used materials handed down from past collectors and scribes, casting them into a new form for a contemporary audience. The writer could also hope, even predict, that his or her new production would join that same stream of inherited scribal tradition and be read by future generations. This concern with the future is visible when the Deuteronomistic Historian has Joshua command Israel to instruct posterity about the meaning of the Jordan crossing (Josh 4:6-7, 21-24). This same author describes Solomon anticipating the future use of the temple down through history (1 Kgs 8:31-53).

Therefore, authors consciously intended Israelite historiography to become part of a continuing national tradition. Of course, unlike other types of traditional literature such as saga, legend, or song, historiography was a literate and scribal expression of

Israel's heritage. As tradition, it was intended to be preserved and handed down to succeeding generations, and this posterity now includes us. As present-day readers of the historical books, we find ourselves addressed by them and challenged by their assertions about God and God's relationship to humanity. We cannot simply read them as "mere history." They address us with claims that we must either accept, modify, or reject, but cannot ignore.

INTERPRETING THE HISTORICAL BOOKS

Yet important obstacles to the task of interpretation remain. Between biblical history writing and the modern Western reader "there is a great gulf fixed" (Luke 16:26 KJV). To put it bluntly, the historical books fall short of our standards for history writing. That is not to say that the story they tell is not "historylike." There is after all a chronological framework and a succession of central figures and significant events. The historical books gather up individual stories into larger conceptual frameworks, creating unitary wholes. In places, they can be taken to be reliable sources for what really happened. In spite of this, at least three things set the historical books off from history as we presently understand it.

First, in contrast to modern history writing, Israelite historiography was more of a corporate enterprise than an individual achievement. The historical books are the collective and anonymous products of a whole culture rather than the particular work of a few creative individuals. They depend on earlier sources and were reedited and supplemented by numerous later contributors. Admittedly, sometimes a single profound intellect seems to stand behind a work. This appears to be the case with the Throne Succession Story and the Nehemiah Memorial (see the foregoing discussion). Nevertheless, both of these writings have come down to us only as parts of larger works. Biblical historiography is a cultural artifact, produced by many contributors working over several generations. To return to Huizinga's definition of historiography, the historical books represent a "form in which a civilization renders account to itself." In other words, it is a group effort.

Modern readers encounter a second difficulty in understanding the historical books. Unlike modern historians, their authors never seem to evaluate or weigh their sources. The biblical writers freely used both traditional oral lore and earlier scribal works, but contented themselves with these secondary sources. They did not go directly back to archives or other primary sources the way any modern historian would attempt to do. Of course, some of the sources they used appear to have provided them with reliable data. Widely accepted examples of such trustworthy information are administrative lists such as those found in 1 Kings 4:2-19 and Ezra 2 or geographical catalogs such as Joshua 15:20-62 and 18:21-28. Other probably reliable sources stand behind the rosters of David's officials and heroes (2 Sam 8:16-18; 20:23-26; 23:8-39), the inventory of those who rebuilt the wall of Jerusalem (Nehemiah 3), and most of the other lists in Ezra-Nehemiah (Ezra 8:1-14; 10:18-44; Neh 11:3-36; 12:1-26). Joshua contains tribal boundary descriptions with some historical value, and Chronicles preserves possibly reliable lists of fortifications (for example, 2 Chr 11:5-10). Some of this dependable information was apparently derived from inscriptions and official annals (for example, 1 Kgs 14:25-28 and 2 Kgs 20:20), although not directly by the biblical historians. Certain poetic materials are older than the prose accounts that contain them and can provide valuable historical insights. Joshua 10:12-13 and Judges 5 are examples of such ancient poetry.

Nevertheless, many if not most of the sources used by the biblical historiographers cannot be accepted as trustworthy for direct historical reconstruction. Legends, miracle stories, and folktales of all sorts were used without critical evaluation. The operative principle seems to have been to include whatever supported the theological point being made. After all, in a traditional society, one rarely questions tradition. In interpreting the historical books, it is important to remember that no ancient source outside Israel mentions any Old Testament event or personality until the ninth century BCE.

The third great obstacle to understanding originates from our modern perceptions about cause and effect. As already mentioned, the system of causation operative in Old Testament historiography is centered on God and God's will. Although there is some recognition of psychological (1 Kgs 1:6), social (1 Kgs 12:4), or geopolitical (Judg 18:27-28; 2 Kgs 17:4) factors, in the last analysis it is the passions and purposes of the God of Israel that drive history. The goals of these Old Testament historians were expressly theological. They sought to persuade their readers to think a certain way about themselves and their relationship to God. Consequently, the historical books are best understood as kerygmatic history, that is "preached history."

Despite being kerygmatic history, however, the Old Testament historical books remain genuine historiography. They are still something quite different from works of outright fiction. This is because their authors intended to recount and explain the past as they encountered it in their sources. Their sources may not have been completely trustworthy, but these writers were not engaged in simply making up convenient stories. Even history writing that is thoroughly biased and largely wrong is not the same thing as fiction. It is not fiction because it intends to be about reality and because it is dependent on sources of some kind. Historiography is referential literature. It points to a subject outside itself, namely the past as the writer thinks it took place. Historiography aims to be accurate about its representation of the past, to arrange it properly or meaningfully, and to evaluate incidents truthfully as to their importance and significance. The Old Testament historian (as opposed to the mere storyteller) intended to refer and claimed to refer to real people and real events, even if we moderns may sometimes question their authenticity.[11]

CHAPTER 2

THE HISTORICAL CONTEXT

When an interpreter reads one of the historical books, the notion of historical context works at two levels. Naturally, the reader needs to take into account the period described in the historiographic narrative. This first context is the period that is the topic of the work, its historical subject. At the same time, the reader must bear in mind that the actual composition of the historiographic narrative generally took place at a later period. In fact, the process of writing and editing most likely stretched out over several generations. This means that the reader must be aware of two or more historical contexts at the same time. As an analogy, consider Charles Dickens' historical novel *A Tale of Two Cities*. The thoughtful reader must take into account both the background of the French Revolution, which is the subject of the story (1789), and the author's own historical period, Victorian England (1859).

All the historical books were composed and achieved their final form in periods considerably later than the events they portray.

The books that describe Israel's emergence in the land (Joshua, Judges) and the period of becoming a nation state (1 and 2 Samuel) first developed as written literature only in the period of the monarchy. First and 2 Kings and 1 and 2 Chronicles, which describe the monarchy, did not achieve their final form until the exilic and postexilic periods respectively.

ISRAEL'S EMERGENCE (JOSHUA, JUDGES)

Israel first appears on the stage of verifiable history about 1210 BCE. A monument erected by the Egyptian Pharaoh Merneptah identifies Israel as a people living in the land of Canaan. Israel's tradition spoke of being descended from ancestors who had once lived in the land of Canaan, but who had migrated to Egypt and become slaves there. These traditions also asserted that Israel later escaped from Egyptian slavery and invaded Canaan to seize it from its former inhabitants. However, no independent historical evidence supports any of these accounts. In fact, recent archaeological study indicates that Israel never actually invaded Canaan from the outside, and certainly not in the unified, massive way described in the book of Joshua.

The books of Joshua and Judges depend on later traditions about Israel's origin and national identity, rather than on genuine memories of an invasion and conquest. These books gathered together folktales that had been originally told about small, individual groups and their local heroes. Scholars have been able to use these folktales to reconstruct the history of Israel's growing national selfconsciousness. However, they offer little trustworthy data for the task of reconstructing Israel's emergence as a distinct group in Palestine. What little can be said with any assurance about this early period has been pieced together from archaeology and from sociological comparisons with other peoples experiencing similar cultural situations.[1]

According to archaeologists, the origin of Israel can be associated with the rapid growth of a large number of small, unfortified settlements in the central hill country during the late thirteenth and early twelfth centuries (the 1200s and 1100s BCE). These new villages apparently came into being because of a breakdown in the cultural and political conditions that had existed in Canaan for centuries.

31

Palestine had long been divided into small city-states under Egyptian domination. Each was governed by a local king and dominated by a military aristocracy. Over time, Egyptian tax demands and political maneuvering led to the weakening of this city-state structure and the disintegration of its economy. At the close of the thirteenth century, Egypt had fallen into weakness and anarchy and was no longer a controlling presence in Palestine. In those unsettled times, ordinary peasant farmers would have suffered great hardship. The burden of taxation naturally fell most heavily on them. They were required to provide forced labor on state construction projects. Peasants living in exposed villages would find themselves unprotected in times of civil unrest and war.

Many scholars believe that the increasing weakness of the Canaanite city-states provided these oppressed peasants with an opportunity to shape a new life for themselves in new locations. As the power of those urban centers waned, peasant farmers and herders may have repudiated their relationships with their former overlords and sought an independent life in the highlands. New farming settlements blossomed in the previously unpopulated highlands of Palestine, away from the authority of the aristocratic lowland cities. The balance of economic and political power gradually began to shift away from Palestine's older urban culture to these new rural settlements. Scholars increasingly identify these new settlements with the people of Israel. These Israelite settlers were not outside invaders as biblical tradition declares. Rather they were indigenous pioneers attracted by new agricultural opportunities and seeking to escape from the economic and political domination of the Canaanite city-states.

The actual details of Israel's origin remain unknown, but a violent invasion or even a peaceful infiltration from the outside appears unlikely. The material culture of the Israelite highland settlements was fundamentally similar to that of the older Canaanite lowland urban centers. For example, the pottery found in these highland villages is essentially the same as that found in the cities and continues the pottery tradition of the previous centuries without any break. Admittedly, some cities in Palestine did suffer military destruction at this time, among them Bethel, Lachish, and Hazor. However, the inventory of cities actually destroyed does not correlate very well with what the book of Joshua reports about Israel's military victories. In fact, any num-

32

ber of hostile forces could have destroyed these cities. The Egyptians and the invading Sea Peoples (Philistines and related ethnic groups) are likely possibilities. Moreover, the new Israelite settlements rarely appeared on the sites of destroyed cities, but rather in previously unsettled rural territory.

Thus in the period before Israel was organized into a monarchical state, the land of Canaan was home to two cultural systems existing side by side. In the lowlands and in a few highland locations, the long-established urban culture of the Canaanite cities continued. These cities were ruled by local kings and protected by walls and chariots. At the same time, an alternative social system of unwalled rural villages had grown up in the hill country of Galilee and central Palestine. These small settlements supported themselves by farming and herding, tilling land that had not previously been under cultivation. These pioneers were able to make good use of previously existing technologies to exploit the hill country environment successfully. Chief among these practices were terrace farming, secure methods of grain storage, and the construction of underground cisterns lined with lime plaster. The houses in these villages were all of similar size and built in a similar style. There were no public buildings or larger dwellings for an elite governing class. This suggests that early Israel had an uncomplicated social structure without significant differences in status or wealth. The stories preserved in the book of Judges seem to reflect accurately the egalitarian society that characterized the early stages of Israel's development. Eventually, many of these settlements were abandoned, as the political center of gravity once more returned to urban culture in the later monarchy period.

These parallel "Canaanite" and "Israelite" cultures shared the same language and even many similar ideas about religion. One important difference was political structure. Canaan was organized by state structures such as kingship, taxes, and military coercion. Early Israel operated instead on the basis of family and clan kinship structures and a shared sense of social solidarity.

Extended families saw themselves as members of clans, which were larger social units understood as reflecting common descent. Marriage normally took place within one's own clan. Clans in geographical proximity to one another gradually coalesced into tribes. These tribes evolved in order to provide a source of mutual protection for the families and clans that constituted them. Certain tribes (Judah, Ephraim, and Benjamin) took the name of their geographic locale. Issachar ("hired worker"; Gen 49:14-15) appears to have been named for its low status as a tribe of serfs or vassal servants. Some clans shifted their membership from one tribe to another over time.

At first, most Israelites probably felt little or no sense of identity beyond the horizon of their family, clan, and tribe. However, eventually a sense of national affinity emerged, based on shared cultural values and common social and economic structures. The very old Song of Deborah (Judges 5) witnesses to some sense of military obligation going beyond allegiance solely to one's own tribe. This song and other ancient poetic texts (for example, Exodus 15) suggest that the tribes' emerging sense of national unity developed out of an incessant need to fend off belligerent neighboring peoples. Another unifying factor was their shared allegiance to their God Yahweh, who fought for them as a divine warrior. The traditional stories that lie behind the books of Joshua and Judges reflect this early stage of Israel's gradual consolidation and developing sense of identity.

The book of Joshua preserves earlier stories of a conquest of Canaan under the leadership of Yahweh. These narratives had circulated by word of mouth as oral tradition in Israel long before they were collected and written down in the monarchical period. Israel used these narratives to construct and strengthen its national identity. These conquest traditions also explained various features of the Palestinian landscape, especially why it was dotted with numerous city ruins such as Jericho, Ai, and Hazor (Joshua 6, 8, 11). They also provided explanations for the continued presence of foreign groups in Israel such as the descendants of Rahab or the Gibeonites (Joshua 2, 9). Thus, emerging Israel was able to discover and reinforce its developing ethnic identity by telling stories of victorious conquest.

The heroic tales preserved in the book of Judges served a similar purpose. Hostile peoples surrounded and threatened developing Israel. These groups sometimes sought to dominate Israel and appropriate its land. Among them were the Canaanite city-states with their military aristocracies and chariot forces. To the east were Ammon and Moab, as well as desert raiders like the Midianites.

In the long term, however, the most serious threat came from the Philistines. Along with other related groups (collectively known as the Sea Peoples), they had moved southward into the eastern Mediterranean from their original homeland around the Aegean Sea. This migration took place about the same time as Israel began to emerge as a distinct people. After attacks on Egypt, the Philistines settled on the southern coast of Canaan. Much later the Greeks and Romans would designate the whole land of Canaan as Palestine, a name derived from "Philistine." Organized into a confederation of five cities, they began to dominate southern and central Israel. They even established garrisons at important points deep in Israelite territory (1 Sam 10:5). The tradition behind 1 Samuel 13:19-22 recalls their technical superiority and political dominance over their less sophisticated Israelite neighbors. Philistine ascendancy lasted until the reign of David.

Local struggles against these various hostile groups gave rise to tales of heroic military leaders such as Ehud, Deborah, Gideon, and Jephthah (Judges 3–12) or individual champions like Samson (Judges 13–16). Retelling these inspiring stories gave beleaguered Israel confidence and courage in their struggles with their neighbors. Eventually these local figures evolved into national heroes. As such, they served as the raw material for the later creation of the book of Judges.

STATE BUILDING (1 AND 2 SAMUEL)

This period covers roughly the eleventh and early tenth centuries (the 1000s and early 900s).[2] The pattern of Israel's settlement, scattered about in the highlands, was not favorable to the development of national unity. The wide Jezreel Valley formed a zone of Canaanite control that divided southern Galilee from the central highlands of Ephraim and Manasseh. The city of Jerusalem and its approaches from the west created a second barrier. This wedge split the southern tribe of Judah off from the rest of Israel. Judah's distinctive identity continued to play a divisive role in Israel's history, leading not only to the division of Solomon's united kingdom, but to controversies in the postexilic period. The Jordan River formed another barrier, although more psychological than physical. The incident reported in

Judges 12:5-6 witnesses to group rivalries and dialectical differences between groups east and west of the Jordan.

Beyond some shared notions of tribal kinship and loyalty to Yahweh as a common God, Israel seems to have had no central institutions in the premonarchy period. Yahweh was worshiped at numerous local sites rather than at a central national shrine. There certainly were ties of an economic and commercial nature between Israel's different regions, but no central authority. Government meant nothing more extensive than the local political structures of clan and village elders. Some early texts also speak of elders on the tribal level (Judg 11:5; 1 Sam 30:26).

As long as Israel remained a loose affiliation of clans and tribes without an effective centralized administration, its ability to resist foreign incursions or domination was limited. The Song of Deborah (Judges 5) describes what must have been a typical state of affairs. Of the ten tribal groups that might be expected to join in battle against the Canaanite kings, only six responded. It seems likely that it was principally the threat of Philistine domination that galvanized Israel into adopting kingship as a more effective form of political organization. Archaeology suggests that another source of pressure was a large population increase in Israel's hill country. A demand for more arable land may have driven Israel into expanding its settlement into territory claimed by other peoples. Much of this expansion would have taken place in the coastal plain and the Jezreel Valley at the expense of the old Canaanite city-states (Josh 17:14-18) and on the east side of the Jordan (the situation lying behind Judg 11:12-28). Apparently the east Jordan nations of Moab, Ammon, and Edom, while culturally similar to Israel, made the transition to kingship before Israel did.

The stories used to compose Judges and 1 Samuel describe Israel's transition from a decentralized social organization to centralized kingship. What these stories have to say about events and individuals is of uncertain historical value. However, the general picture they reflect—halting first steps, conservative resistance, and repeated failure—is unquestionably accurate. Based on what we know of similar cultures undergoing a transition to monarchic state, the biblical story at least approximates historical reality. Local chieftains would have exercised control over limited

36

areas. Gideon in Manasseh (Judges 6–8) and Jephthah in Gilead (Judges 11–12) are examples remembered by tradition. At times, there would be attempts to establish a dynasty and to prolong the power of a chieftain's family into the next generation. As an example, Judges 9 describes Abimelech, son of the military hero Gideon, establishing and trying to defend a short-lived local monarchy centered on the city-state of Shechem.

Saul was remembered as Israel's first king, but in some ways tradition portrays him as a chieftain figure similar to Gideon or Jephthah. He was famed as a successful military leader against the encroaching Ammonite kingdom and raiding Amalekites. His success with the imperialistic Philistines was mixed, and tradition reports his self-inflicted death in a climactic defeat by the Philistines at Mount Gilboa. His son Esh-baal (or Ish-bosheth, NRSV "Ishbaal") reigned after him for a brief period, but apparently only over a much-reduced area.

David's success capped these earlier attempts at permanent kingship. Traditions preserved and edited largely by David's supporters and descendants portray him as an opportunistic adventurer who emerged from Saul's royal court to chart an independent course as a mercenary and populist leader. No doubt, these sources may be trusted in reporting that David first began as king of Judah only, reigning from the regional capital of Hebron. The assassination of Saul's successor led to an invitation to rule as king over both Judah and Israel. The tradition that David captured Jerusalem from its indigenous inhabitants is also likely to be reliable. This achievement provided him with a prestigious capital city. It strengthened the new centralized monarchy by giving it a home power base unconnected with traditional tribal structures, territory, or loyalties. Later generations turned David into a hero on a grand scale, recounting how he turned the tables on their former enemies, neutralizing the Philistines and absorbing Ammon, Moab, and Edom. Actually, David probably reigned with only limited governmental apparatus over what was still largely a decentralized nation. One list that may possibly survive from his reign is a catalog of military heroes (2 Sam 23:8-39).

Kingship naturally implies both dynastic rule and dynastic quarrels. Second Samuel 9–20 and 1 Kings 1–2 describe a convoluted power struggle among David's sons to succeed to his throne. Solomon, one of David's younger sons, was the eventual victor and inherited the kingdom. These chapters constitute what scholars call the "Throne Succession Story" (see chapter 7), a work that sounds remarkably like a modern historical novel. This historiographic work is of uncertain date, and scholars differ concerning its credibility as a historical source. David and his direct descendants reigned as kings from Jerusalem for four centuries, from a little after 1000 to 586 BCE. Both the Bible and an extrabiblical source refer to Judah and its ruling family as "the house of David."

MONARCHY (1 AND 2 KINGS, 1 AND 2 CHRONICLES)

The Old Testament is our chief source for the history of Israel's monarchy (sometimes called the First Temple period), although extrabiblical inscriptions provide some supportive data. This period incorporates the tenth up to a little after the end of the seventh century (900s through the 600s). Although the books of Kings and Chronicles interpret events in a thoroughly theocentric and theological way, they frequently use sources that furnish useful historical details. Because the chronologies given in these books contain serious internal discrepancies, the dates offered by scholars for events and individual reigns are usually only approximate. Sometimes extrabiblical sources can provide more exact dates and alternative perspectives.

Solomon solidly established a monarchy centered on Jerusalem that would last for centuries, although the short-lived union of Judah with the rest of Israel dissolved after his death. Materials of varied historical worth have been preserved in the "Book of the Acts of Solomon," the source lying behind much of 1 Kings 3–11 (1 Kgs 11:41; see chap. 8). This literary work extolled Solomon and narrated his attempts to build a strong centralized monarchy. A list of his administrative officers (4:2-19) reveals a division of the kingdom into twelve districts. This arrangement excluded Judah and consequently continued to maintain its distinct status within greater Israel. Some of these new districts followed tribal lines, but supplanted tribal structures with royal officials. The configuration of other districts shows that Solomon incorporated the former Canaanite city-states into his realm, creating a multiethnic nation-state.

Following the tradition of other ancient kings, Solomon increased the strength and prestige of his throne by constructing military installations (9:15-19) and royal buildings (7:1-8), including a state temple in Jerusalem. These building projects required the use of forced labor that Solomon demanded from both his Canaanite and Israelite subjects (5:13-18; 9:20-22). He negotiated foreign alliances, securing them by diplomatic marriages (3:1) and engaged in lucrative foreign trade (9:26-28; 10:22, 28-29). On the negative side, Edom and Syria resisted Israelite rule (11:14-25), and Solomon reportedly had to give up some territory in Galilee (9:10-13).

Some of the material presented in the book of Kings can be assigned to the two other written sources it cites. These are the "Book of the Annals of the Kings of Israel" and the "Book of the Annals of the Kings of Judah." These accounts provided information on wars, conspiracies, and building projects. They seem to have been literary works based on inscriptions and other official sources. They also seem to have provided the author of Kings with the order of succession and duration of reign for the kings of each kingdom. Extrabiblical documents and inscriptions provide important additional information and broadly corroborate the outline of events offered by Kings.[3] Chronicles, on the other hand, is largely dependent on Kings and only rarely provides additional information of historical value.

The somewhat artificial union of Judah with the rest of Israel dissolved after Solomon's death, resulting in two small kingdoms that coexisted for about two centuries. In addition to the tribal territory of Judah, the southern Davidic kingdom also included Jerusalem, which continued to maintain a degree of administrative distinctiveness, and a region in the territory of Benjamin extending a few miles north of the capital. The rival kingdom of Israel encompassed all the rest, including a number of former Canaanite cities. Israel was definitely the richer, more powerful, and more cosmopolitan of the two kingdoms. Bethel and Dan served as national sanctuaries under royal sponsorship. Jeroboam, the founder of the Northern Kingdom, was not able to establish a solid dynastic succession. However, successful dynasties were later established during the ninth and early eighth centuries, first by Omri and then by Jehu. With the exception of these two dynasties, Israel experienced continuous political instability, including seven royal assassinations and a suicide. By contrast, Judah enjoyed the relative stability of a single ruling family, although coups and royal assassinations did take place. These resulted largely from disagreements over national policy.

Although both kingdoms worshiped Yahweh as their national god, popular religious thought and practice was much more diverse than the reader of the Old Testament might assume. Later biblical composers and editors made the religious practices that eventually prevailed in the postexilic period the paradigm for preexilic orthodoxy. However, both archaeology and hints submerged within the Old Testament itself reveal a more varied picture. Loyalty to Yahweh did not yet exclude the belief that other gods existed and were active. Popular religion continued to venerate deities who were involved with agricultural and household matters. It is likely that women expressed their own religious aspirations apart from the male-dominated public worship of Yahweh. Archaeologists frequently uncover female figurines in Israelite sites, indicating an intense concern for personal fertility and childbirth. Two inscriptions from the divided monarchy period indicate that some Israelites venerated the goddess Asherah as Yahweh's consort. Archaeologists have also discovered an open-air worship site or "high place" in the north central hill country that featured a standing stone and the bronze statuette of a bull.

Archaeology indicates that the ninth century was a period of prosperity for both kingdoms, but that economic decline characterized the eighth and seventh centuries. A growing concentration of wealth in the hands of a small lending class resulted in a growing gap between the rich and poor and the economic oppression of the peasants. Those who could not pay their debts commonly had to sell themselves into slavery (2 Kgs 4:1; Amos 2:6; 8:6). The tax burden was increased by defensive wars (for example, Israel against Assyria and Aram), campaigns to recover lost subject states (Israel in Moab, Judah in Edom), and eventually the payment of heavy tribute to Assyria (for example, 2 Kgs 15:19-20). Noteworthy events from the late–tenth century to the middle of the eighth include:

• The invasion of Palestine by the Egyptian king Shishak (1 Kgs 14:25-28), who recorded his campaign on a temple wall in Egypt and set up a victory monument in Megiddo (about 920 BCE).
• Omri of Israel established a stable dynasty, made Samaria the capital of Israel, and recaptured Moab (the early ninth century; 1 Kgs 16:21-28 and the Mesha Inscription).
• Omri's son Ahab of Israel led a coalition of small states against the Assyrians at Qarqar (853 BCE; Assyrian sources) and lost Moab (Mesha Inscription).
• Jehu established a new dynasty in Israel through a bloody purge (about 843; 2 Kings 9–10) and paid tribute to Assyria (in 841 BCE according to Assyrian sources). During his coup, he assassinated the king of Judah, whose mother Athaliah then seized the throne of Judah (2 Kgs 11:1-3).
• Athaliah was assassinated and replaced by Joash, allegedly the legitimate heir to Judah's throne (about 837; 2 Kgs 11:4-21).
• The contemporaries Jeroboam II of Israel and Azariah (or Uzziah) of Judah reigned over a final period of peace and prosperity (early eighth century; 2 Kgs 14:23–15:7).

Events triggered by the reappearance of an aggressive Assyria dominated the history of Israel and Judah from the middle of the eighth century until the close of the seventh. Assyria destroyed and absorbed Israel completely, although Judah was able to survive as an Assyrian vassal state. Important historical developments in this period include:

• Jeroboam II's son, the last member of the Jehu dynasty, was assassinated. Menahem of Israel paid heavy tribute to Assyria (about 737; 2 Kgs 15:19-20).
• After assassinating Menahem's son, Pekah of Israel combined with the king of Aram (Syria) in a rebellious coalition against Assyria. These two tried to intimidate Ahaz of Judah into joining. This so-called Syro-Ephraimite War resulted in an Assyrian assault that left Israel with only a fraction of its original territory, centered on its capital, Samaria (734–732; 2 Kgs 15:29; 16:5-9).
• Hoshea, the last king of Israel, rebelled against Assyria. The Assyrians captured Samaria and incorporated what was left of Israel into the Assyrian state (722; 2 Kgs 17:3-6).

The Assyrians turned the former state of Israel into four provinces of the Assyrian Empire (Dor, Megiddo, and Gilead in 732 BCE, and Samaria after 722). Judah was able to continue a precarious independent existence as a satellite state by paying annual tribute.

• Judah's king Hezekiah attempted a chancy rebellion against Assyria (in 701) and was lucky to escape with his throne and the city of Jerusalem intact (2 Kings 18–19). The Assyrian king Sennacherib vividly records the destruction of the city of Lachish in palace wall reliefs and reports that he seized parts of Judah's territory.
• King Manasseh loyally paid tribute to Assyria and enjoyed a long reign (2 Kings 21). His son was assassinated and replaced by his grandson Josiah (in 640; 2 Kgs 21:23-24).

As Assyria began to weaken before the reawakening power of Egypt and Babylon, Judah enjoyed a brief period of national expansion and independent action under Josiah. The book of Kings attributes to Josiah a religious reform inspired by the rediscovery of "the book of the law of Moses" (that is, Deuteronomy; 2 Kings 22–23). In accordance with this law (Deuteronomy 12), Josiah closed all local Yahweh sanctuaries and centralized all sacrificial worship in the Jerusalem Temple (622 BCE).

• Josiah died at the hand of the Egyptian Pharaoh Neco under mysterious circumstances (in 609; 2 Kgs 23:28-30). Egypt and Babylon struggled with each other to inherit the imperial legacy of Assyria, and Judah found itself caught in the middle.
• After two unsuccessful revolts against the new Babylonian Empire (597 and 586), Jerusalem was devastated and its temple was demolished (2 Kings 24–25).

After each rebellion, the Babylonians deported substantial numbers of Judah's intelligentsia and ruling class into exile. Among them was Judah's next-to-last king, Jehoiachin, considered by most to be the true heir to the throne. A third exile followed in 581 BCE after the assassination of Gedaliah, whom the Babylonians had appointed to administer Judah (2 Kgs 25:22-26). Most of the ordinary people remained behind in Judah.

RESTORATION (EZRA, NEHEMIAH)

The life of these exiles in Babylonian territories does not seem to have been particularly inhumane. Some Judahites (Jews) were settled on agricultural reclamation projects. Others eventually became involved in commercial activities. Jews also settled in Egypt during the exilic period. These Jewish expatriates were generally able to retain their traditional customs and religion. Life also went on for those who remained in Palestine, where the worship of Yahweh continued at the site of the former Jerusalem Temple. North of Judah, people descended from the population of the former kingdom of Israel also continued to worship Yahweh. The Babylonian Empire collapsed with the capture of Babylon by Cyrus (539 BCE). It was replaced by the Persian Empire, which endured for about two centuries.

Under the relatively more benevolent policies of Cyrus and his successors, Jewish leadership classes began a gradual process of return to Judah. The book of Ezra-Nehemiah describes this period of reconstruction, which took place in the last part of the sixth and first part of the fifth centuries (roughly 540 to 430 BCE). Ezra-Nehemiah is highly ideological in its presentation and historically confused in places. It sometimes telescopes and confuses events and personalities from different periods. Some have even suggested that it reverses the order of its two main characters, Ezra and Nehemiah! Not surprisingly, scholars have found it difficult to reconstruct a coherent picture of the restoration period.

• The Jerusalem Temple was rebuilt and rededicated (in 515) under the leadership of the Persian appointee Zerubbabel and the high priest Joshua (Ezra 3–6). This began the Second Temple period, which ended in 70 CE with the Roman destruction of a renovated version of this temple.
• The priest Ezra proclaimed the version of Jewish religious law current among the exiles and enforced it on the populace of Judah. He did this as an agent of the Persian king Artaxerxes (Ezra 7–10, Nehemiah 8–10). Depending on which Artaxerxes was involved, Ezra's mission began in either 458 or 398.
• The Persians appointed the Jewish official Nehemiah as gover-

nor (445). He rebuilt the city wall and resettled rural villagers in the city (Nehemiah 1–6, 11–13).

The exilic and early postexilic eras were highly creative times. Much of the Old Testament originated or reached its final form in the exilic and Persian periods. Unfortunately, we know little about the events, parties, and controversies that shaped the history of the Persian province of Judah.

CHAPTER 3

PATTERNS OF READING

THE ART OF INTERPRETATION

The historiographic or historylike narratives of the Old Testament may be read in a naive and surface way, just as one might read the morning paper. What is reported may be simply understood as what actually happened. In this sort of reading, the issue of "meaning" is reduced to merely following the story line, or at best discovering some moral lesson. Such a surface reading rarely trips over difficulties in the text, but instead blithely ignores them. This is a typical way of reading texts because the human mind routinely skips over irregularities and inconsistencies, unconsciously filling in blanks. The reader untrained in the art of interpretation often fails to read the words that actually make up the text. Instead, what is "read" turns out to be what the reader's mind has generated out of a selective perception of the text's raw materials. We read the text that is in our mind rather than the text that is on the page.

In order to come to terms with a biblical text in a disciplined way, it is first necessary to pay attention to the words that are actually on the page. That is to say, the reading process must be slowed down and made more deliberate and purposeful. Because we live in a culture in which rapid reading and quick skimming are vital survival skills, this process of "slow reading" or "close reading" must be learned by practice. A reader becomes an interpreter when such a slowed, questioning, disciplined, attentive act of reading takes place. As an interpreter, one pays attention to a text's effect on oneself as reader and tries to predict its likely effect on others. One moves on to become a *public* interpreter when a larger audience is invited into the act of reading. In speaking, teaching, or writing about a text, the public interpreter performs an act of bridge building between text and its new audience. The disciplined use of critical interpretative methodologies helps to make these private and public acts of interpretation fruitful and responsible.

Most modern texts spring from a single author at a single time. In contrast, biblical texts are rarely one-dimensional or flat in this sense. They are usually the products of composite authorship over a period of centuries. Such texts do not simply offer the views and perspectives of an individual or even a generation, but of a whole people over several generations. Often the process of composition reaches back into a period of oral tradition. Stories, sayings, songs, and laws were composed orally and passed down by word of mouth for generations before being written down. Even after being originally composed, biblical texts often continued to change, as later generations of readers and copyists continued to modify them.

Consequently, the historical books of the Old Testament communicate to their readers with many voices speaking out of a complex matrix of relationships. Naturally, what these books have to say correlates to a greater or lesser degree with the facts of the history they are reporting. However, they also reflect the complex history of their own formation and the concerns of the various audiences that have preserved and modified them over the centuries. These are not "flat" texts with only a single dimension of meaning. Rather they speak with a lively resonance because they echo the history of so many diverse periods, concerns, and convictions. They scintillate as multilayered stories told from more than one perspective at once.

For these reasons, the historical books require a lot from their readers. They are the sort of texts that demand disciplined work and conscious effort. The interpreter must wrestle with such texts in order to comprehend them. This wrestling metaphor implies that what the text has to say to the reader is slippery and must be resolutely grasped. However, it also suggests that the act of reading is a two-way transaction in which both text and reader are involved. On the one hand, these texts engage their present-day readers actively. They challenge, preach, warn, entertain, explain, confront, convert, comfort, and uplift. On the other hand, the reader brings much to the interpretative arena in the way of concerns, questions, presuppositions, and expectations. The well-informed interpreter also brings historical knowledge and critical skills. This interaction between dynamic text and alert reader creates new worlds of meaning. Biblical interpretation or exegesis is the exploration of this two-sided process of meaning creation in which both text and reader take an active part.

In spite of the negative connotations often associated with the word "criticism," biblical criticism is not a hostile attack on the Bible's integrity. Rather, the various interpretative methodologies used by biblical scholars offer the reader ways to pry apart the intricate tangle of voices and superimposed layers of meaning that characterize biblical texts. They provide disciplined approaches to the task of discovering the relationships between a text's various components and their interdependence. They also give the reader a variety of places to stand in order to view the text from different perspectives.[1]

Some of these methods are historical in outlook. They seek out the facts of the history being narrated. They endeavor to uncover the history of the text's development. They try to clarify the story of the text's interaction with successive audiences and communities of faith over time. These interpretative methods are sometimes called diachronic, from the Greek "through time." Other methods are synchronic ("at the same time"). These techniques of interpretation ignore historical matters and concentrate instead on the internal relationships of the elements of the text to one another, to other texts in the same canon, and to the reader in the act of reading. The story of the history behind the text or out of which the text has arisen is set aside in favor of the story that now plays itself out between text and reader. Because the historical books are simultaneously both narrative and historiography, interpreting them responsibly requires both diachronic and synchronic methods.

The story of David's census and the plague that resulted from it will serve as a test case to introduce these critical methodologies. To begin, try reading 2 Samuel 24 one sentence at a time. Pause after each sentence to think about what exactly is being said and, just as important, what is *not* being said. What questions emerge as the text makes its impact on you? Write them down. Noting down puzzles and questions is an excellent discipline for the developing interpreter. Next you might want to read the chapter aloud as a further way of focusing your attention. For most people this process of "slowed reading" will generate a sizable list of questions. Why was the Lord angry in the first place? What is wrong about taking a census? Why did David repent even before his punishment was announced? When did the plague actually stop? What sort of God is represented here? Certainly the statement that the Lord "incited David" to misbehave strikes most readers as perplexing, if not sacrilegious!

READING AS STORY (LITERARY CRITICISM)

Literary criticism is a broad term for the investigation of how a biblical text is shaped in order to have an effect on its reader. The interpreter treats the text in its finished form as a self-contained phenomenon without regard to the history of its origin or the historical events to which it ostensibly refers. Objects of attention include the text's rhetorical strategy, literary style, and organization. Because historiographic texts are almost exclusively narratives, the study of plot and character is important for interpreting the historical books.[2] Narratives are a series of episodes connected together into a plot. A plot begins with a narrative problem and then moves toward a solution to that problem. In all but the simplest plots, the main problem and attempts to react to it generate other problems along the way. These obstacles or subproblems must be dealt with before the narrative can end. Narratives tend to begin with an *exposition* that sets the stage and tells us what is amiss. The narrative *action* then unfolds, and complications arise out of the original problem or attempted

48

solutions to it. The action rises in interest or tension up to the *climax*. This is the moment of greatest reader interest. It is the crisis of decision, the apex of tension, the most intense point in a series of events. The final stage of a plot is the *denouement* in which questions are answered and loose ends tied up. All but the simplest of narratives will have several episodes, each of which contributes to the movement of the whole story. It can be profitable for the interpreter to isolate each individual episode and ask how it contributes to the movement of the story as a whole.

The portrayal of character in Old Testament narrative is not as deep or rich as in modern literature. Writers rarely comment on what a given character is thinking or feeling, but may reveal a little about this through what a character says or does. The disciplined interpreter needs to be careful not to presume emotions or motivations for the characters without warrant from the text itself. Scholarly interpreters disparage this as "psychologizing" the text. When reading Old Testament texts through the lens of literary or narrative criticism, it is important to remember that God is also one of the characters involved in the plot.

In 2 Samuel 24, the primary narrative problem is obvious: "The anger of the LORD was kindled against Israel" (v. 1). The reader is never told why the Lord is angry, and must learn to be content with never finding out. To read some sort of motivation into the text would be to psychologize it. The experienced interpreter soon discovers that it is simply futile to pursue a question about which a text remains stubbornly silent. No matter how important an issue may seem to the interpreter, the text's silence must be honored.

The primary problem of God's anger immediately leads to a secondary one. The Lord "incited David" to count the people. Two puzzles immediately confront the reader that would not have troubled the text's earliest audience. The first is how God could incite David to commit an act and then condemn him for it. Modern readers are usually reluctant to question God's absolute goodness. In contrast, Old Testament writers single-mindedly asserted the Lord's omnipotence over the world and were quite unembarrassed about making God the author of disaster and evil. For example, 1 Kings 22 describes God as causing prophets to speak lies in order to lure a king to his death. The Lord is represented as claiming, "I make weal and create woe" (Isa 45:7). Until late in the Old Testament period, Israel was more concerned about boldly confessing God's unlimited power than carefully safeguarding God's goodness and virtue.

A second puzzle concerns the impropriety of taking a national census. That the census was obviously improper is simply assumed by the narrative. This did not need to be explained to the first readers. The "ransom" demanded by Exodus 30:12 attests that a census was sometimes thought to lead to the danger of a plague. This plague was not so much a divine punishment, but an automatic result of impersonal forces, almost a matter of natural law. For this reason, the harmful effect of David's census had to play itself out even after his initial repentance (v. 10). Since this census counted available military manpower, it was probably also seen as an administrative innovation that encroached on the Lord's established role as the leader of Israel's armies. The episode describing Joab's objection to the census (v. 3) underscores for the reader the problematic nature of David's orders. The folly of this move is clear even to Joab, a character never noted for his piety or morality in the other stories told in 2 Samuel. David's interior motive in taking a census remains hidden; he simply wants to "know how many there are." The reader may wonder whether David acts out of pride or lack of faith, or whether perhaps he is celebrating God's benevolence in granting him such a populous nation. However, again the text's silence about his inner psychological state must be respected. David simply judges it as an act "done very foolishly" (v. 10).[3]

The description of the census itinerary makes it clear that the survey was painstaking and thorough. A committee of commanders carries it out. It is extensive in space (2 Sam 24:5-7) and time (v. 8). The high totals testify both to God's generous grace and to the folly of David's action. He had no need to worry about "how many" (v. 2)![4] From a literary standpoint, the precisely itemized route introduces delay into the plot. Readers anxious to find out what sort of catastrophe the census will bring must first endure the tension of a detailed geography lesson. Slowing a narrative down to increase dramatic tension is a common narrative tactic for increasing reader interest. In addition, the route of the survey commission foreshadows (hints at in anticipation) the course of the plague: Dan, Beersheba, then to Jerusalem (vv. 15-16).

The plague is the next narrative problem. However, the connection between the census and the plague is an indirect one. An act of confession by David brings on an intervening episode of testing (2 Sam 24:11-14), which in turn brings about the pestilence. In other words, v. 10 links vv. 1-9 (census) to vv. 11-16 (penalty). David's repentance and plea in v. 10 does not lead to the end of the story as one might expect. (God forgave him and they lived happily ever after!) Instead, this scene functions as a moment of "discovery," in which a character realizes a truth that moves the plot action forward. We are not told what prompted David to change his mind. Did the huge census figures make him aware of the rich extravagance of God's blessings? Yet, an answer to this question is not really important to our understanding of the narrative. What is significant is that David has discovered what he needs to know in order for the next episode to take place. Consequently, the prophetic messenger Gad does not accuse David, but rather offers him a threefold choice that propels the story forward to the plague episode. The narrative telescopes the reception and delivery of God's message in a fashion typical of Old Testament storytelling. The first part of the communication is revealed to the reader as the Lord talks to Gad (v. 12), and the second part is reported as Gad talks to David (v. 13).

From the viewpoint of literary criticism, this threefold choice introduces more narrative delay, but also serves as a test of David's integrity and a claim about the Lord's character. The precise nature of David's choice is somewhat obscure. The shorter catastrophes seem to be more intense, so that the damage done by any of the three options would be similar.[5] Each would reduce the population that David has been so concerned about and lessen his war-making power. Although they all strike against the whole nation, they are described using the second person singular pronoun.[6] This last observation broaches the delicate topic of solidarity between king and nation that will appear in verse 17. The fate of people depends on the king's relationship to God, and each of these punishments would strike the people more directly than it would strike the king himself.

David's reply in 2 Samuel 24:14 is ambiguous and leaves the reader with unanswered questions. Does he mean only to exclude the option of pursuit by his foes ("human hands")? Alternatively, does he lean toward plague as the choice most directly from God's "hand"? Does he protect himself, while selfishly exposing his subjects to danger (not "me" but "us" in v. 14)? It can be frustrating, but learning to live with unanswerable questions and deliberate ambiguity is an important interpretative skill. Perhaps it is best simply to take David's words at face value, as the text's way of highlighting his faith and piety. He chooses to put himself and his nation into the hands of the One whose "mercy is great."

Verse 15 is a rest point in the narrative, but not the end. Although the pestilence has struck and the "appointed time" has arrived, the fundamental narrative problem of the Lord's anger has not yet reached a solution. Together verses 16-17 move the plot in a new direction. Verse 16 literally "points" the development of the story in the direction of Jerusalem ("stretched out his hand"). The Lord's change of heart illustrates the truth of David's faithful declaration in verse 14: The Lord's mercy is in fact great. With the end of the plague, the story reaches a climax of sorts. However, because the linked problems of divine anger and the Lord's incitement of David to sin have not been resolved definitely, there is still more to come.

David's glimpse of the angel (2 Sam 24:17) moves the plot action from the plague episode to the upcoming story of altar building. The angel strikes with the pestilence, but also serves as a visible signal to the reader to pay attention to the threshing floor. Once David has seen the angel there, it disappears from the narrative. David's second repentance (v. 17) clears up the troubling issue of solidarity between king and people raised earlier by verse 14. David now admits that God ought to direct any further punishment against himself and his family. The prospect of continued punishment again propels the plot one step closer to the construction of the altar by means of Gad's advice and God's command to build an altar (vv. 18-19). Now the effectiveness of this altar becomes a new point of narrative tension. Will it work?

The drawn-out episode of purchase (2 Sam 24:20-24) introduces further narrative delay in order to build dramatic suspense. It also functions as a sort of deed, emphasizing that the site of the altar undeniably belongs to Israel and its king and no longer to its former owner. The mysterious figure of Araunah, with his exotic, non-Israelite name, anchors the threshing floor in Jerusalem's past, but his courtly subservience and willingness to transfer ownership defines it as part of Israel's current heritage. The reader is likely to be puzzled, because Gad's words in verse 18 did not spell out what the purpose of this altar was to be. Are the sacrifices to be in thanksgiving that the pestilence has ended? It is only verse 21 that reveals the irony of David's position to the reader. Although the reader already knows that the plague has been halted (v. 16), ironically David knows nothing of the kind.

With verse 25 the plot reaches closure. David's unsettled relationship with the Lord, who incited him to sin, has ceased to be a problem. In addition, the problem of the vicious plague is solved, with three strikes against it. It has run its course (v. 15), been halted by divine command (v. 16), and now averted by proper sacrifice (vv. 21, 25)! Most important, the primary narrative problem of the Lord's anger is no longer an issue: "The Lord answered."

Plot is not the only structural element that can be analyzed in narratives. Another is point of view. A productive way to read this story is to consider the interplay between contrasting divine and human points of view about the same set of events. The story plays out on two levels and follows two schedules. We as readers are aware of both, but the character David is largely ignorant of what is happening on the heavenly plane. From the divine perspective, God is angry, incites David, commissions Gad, sends the pestilence, then repents and stops the plague. On the human plane, David gives orders, discovers his sin, chooses a punishment, repents again, then builds an altar and sacrifices so that the plague can be averted. From God's viewpoint, the plague ceases in verse 16; from David's perspective, it is not over until verse 25. Still, there are contact points between the two realms of the divine and human. Gad is one of these links (vv. 11, 18) and so is the angel. The Lord commands the angel to "stay your hand," and David sees the angel by the threshing floor and repents (vv. 16-17). A third contact point is the threshing floor. It is both the site of God's gracious action to cancel the plague (v. 16) and the location of human rituals intended to appeal to God and to which God responds (v. 25).

READING FOR FORMS (FORM CRITICISM)

Texts and oral literature tend to fall naturally into standard types or *forms*: jokes, letters, instructions, hymns, menus, historiography, and so forth. One of the most fruitful types of biblical criticism identifies such standard forms (or genres), relates them to their appropriate social situations, and seeks to uncover their usual intentions or purposes. Typical genres used by 2 Samuel 24 illustrate form criticism as an interpretive method.

Second Samuel 24:5-7 is an example of a "boundary point list" that has been reused to construct an itinerary. A comparison with texts in Joshua that trace Israel's tribal boundaries indicates that these places once formed a sequence of border points enclosing Israel's territory. In fact, this particular border point list matches data found in Joshua 13:9-11, 16-20; 19:26-29. The writer has borrowed and converted this list into a route for the census commission by providing suitable verbs ("began, came, went out"). Thus, what was once a static description intended to delineate territory has been turned into a dynamic trajectory emphasizing that the census was a thorough job.[7]

Another standard form or genre found in this story is that of the "sanctuary foundation legend." Form critics use the term "legend" to mean an uplifting story about a special person or place. Use of the term does not necessarily make a negative judgment about a story's historicity. Similar examples are Genesis 28:11-22 and Judges 6:11-24. These stories, originally retold by word of mouth, legitimated a given holy place as a proper site for effective sacrifice. Sites for sacrificial altars were thought to be chosen by God (Exod 20:24) and verified by extraordinary visions or experiences. Here the site of Jerusalem's newly founded altar is authorized and endorsed by David's vision of the destroying angel (2 Sam 24:17) and the effectiveness of his sacrifices there (v. 25). Eventually, if not originally, the threshing floor of Araunah was identified with the site of the Jerusalem Temple altar (1 Chr 22:1; 2 Chr 3:1). The retelling of this story was a way of asserting the holiness and effectiveness of the Jerusalem sanctuary.

Some scholars have theorized that this particular sanctuary foundation legend had originally been told by the pre-Israelite inhabitants of Jerusalem (the Jebusites) and that the site of David's altar was an earlier holy place taken over from them. This theory goes on to suggest that the angelic apparition originally represented a Jebusite god. At the very least, the non-Israelite name Araunah points to a pre-Israelite association of some sort in this story.

Another somewhat independent element in the narrative is the land purchase account in 2 Samuel 24:21-24. Genesis 23:3-16 presents a similar dialogue between seller and purchaser. Both texts represent a narrative reuse of the form critical genre "dialogue contract," well known from Babylonian examples. The original purpose of retelling the story of a purchase would have been similar to that of a modern land deed, to certify ownership. Note how the participants' verbal exchange carefully mentions the purchase price and the unambiguous intent to sell and buy. Araunah's initial offer (2 Sam 24:22-23) relates to a common ancient legal fiction that transactions of selling and buying land were really merely exchanges of mutual gifts. The author's reuse of the "dialogue contract" form intends to verify that the holy altar site indisputably does belong to David and thus to his heirs and their subjects. The important Jerusalem sanctuary site is not to be considered Jebusite or foreign, but unquestionably Israelite.

Thus, 2 Samuel 24 contains several recognizable earlier forms or genres. Of these, the "boundary point list" and the "sanctuary foundation legend" unquestionably had an independent existence before being incorporated into this present narrative. To adopt a wider perspective, the form or genre of the entire narrative is that of "historiography," although on a diminutive scale. Similar examples of small-scale history writing are 2 Samuel 9:1-13 and 21:1-14. The genre of historiography explores the meaning and significance of past events of lasting public importance, while attending to questions of cause and effect (see chapter 1). Of course, labeling a narrative "historiography" does not necessarily mean that it or all of its details actually took place. It implies only that the author learned of these events from some source (such as oral tradition or a written document) and believed that they had happened. As is common in biblical historiography, the system of causation in this narrative is primarily theological. Events are driven by the Lord's anger resulting in human sin and the Lord's mercy motivated by human repentance. Much Old Testament historiography about David tends to exhibit a partisan political position by interpreting David's character either favorably (slaying Goliath, 1 Samuel 17) or unfavorably (debauching Bathsheba, 2 Samuel 11). Second Samuel 24 is not so clear on the issue of David's character. His actions are both unworthy (ordering the census) and admirable (building the altar). His faith appears problematic at first (2 Sam 24:14), but eventually shows itself to be exemplary (vv. 17, 24).

READING FOR TRADITIONS (TRADITION HISTORY)

Israel, like any other culture, cherished traditions that expressed their system of belief and their self-understanding. Over time these traditions were modified and expanded to meet changing needs and experiences. Tradition history seeks to describe how the development of Israel's core traditions is reflected in biblical texts. Often such changes in outlook can be traced by comparing older and younger materials found within the same text. At other times, a given text may represent a "snapshot" of one stage in the changing tradition, one that only becomes discernible when compared with other texts.

One tradition pivotal to Judah's self-understanding was the Zion tradition. This is the concept that the Lord had specifically chosen Jerusalem to be the place of special divine presence and that as a consequence Jerusalem was safe from any threatening danger. Many texts reflect this idea, for instance Psalm 46 and 2 Kings 18–19. Judah's traditions asserted God's election of Jerusalem in several parallel ways. Abraham, for example, worshiped at Jerusalem (Salem; Gen 14:17-24), and the ark ended up there after its roundabout journey (2 Sam 6:1-15). Furthermore, the Lord's visible glory pervaded the Jerusalem Temple at its dedication (1 Kgs 8:10-13). Second Samuel chapter 24 represents what may be a somewhat earlier form of this Zion tradition. Here Jerusalem's special divine election rests on the Lord's gracious ending of a deadly plague just before it struck the city, David's vision of the angel, and the effectiveness of sacrifice offered at the city's holy place.

Another important tradition was the theology of the divine warrior. This was the ancient notion that the Lord was a warrior God (compare Exod 15:1-3) who fought to protect Israel and advance its national interests. In wars fought under the leadership of the Lord as divine warrior, the size of Israel's human army was immaterial. The Lord could give victory "by many or by few" (1 Sam 14:6). Not surprisingly, this tradition largely disappeared when kingship appeared and warfare became the province of the king. In the absence of the triumphant divine warrior, the question of David's census—how many could "draw the sword" (2 Sam 24:9)—became critical. The census narrative of 2 Samuel 24 depicts a stage in Israel's thought when the divine warrior tradition is something to be maintained in ideology (the position of Joab, v. 3), but beginning to be disregarded in actual state policy. This narrative still understands the new measures required by royal leadership as apostate acts that sabotage ancient tradition.

Elements of prophetic tradition also emerge in this narrative. As one who conveys messages from God and even back to God (2 Sam 24:13), Gad functions in the traditional prophetic role of divine messenger, using the so-called messenger formula, "thus says the LORD" (v. 12). He also serves as a royal advisor (compare Nathan or Isaiah), delivering the Lord's commands (vv. 18-19). The threefold choice of war, hunger, and pestilence manifests a tradition of divine punishment known from the classical prophets (e.g., Jer 14:12; 15:2). What is not yet present in this narrative is the tradition of prophetic confrontation, judgment, and threat. Gad simply provides David with information; he does not confront the king with a call for repentance. Gad communicates a choice of punishments rather than proclaiming an announcement of doom. This appears to be a somewhat earlier stage in the conception of prophecy than that represented by the confrontational role found in texts such as 2 Samuel 12:1-15; 1 Kings 14:1-18 or 20:35-43. Gad is appropriately given the title "David's seer" (v. 11), a designation used for earlier forms of the prophetic office (1 Sam 9:9).

READING FOR EDITORIAL OUTLOOK (REDACTION CRITICISM)

Redaction criticism investigates the way a text has been edited (redacted) in the process of reaching its present shape. The interpreter tries to distinguish the final product of editing from its predecessor text. One seeks to uncover the purpose behind whatever modifications and arrangements later editors have made in the text.

The information that the Lord was angry "again" (v. 1) is an example of an editorial connection that attaches this narrative to what has come before. This expression connects 2 Samuel

24:1-25 back to the Lord's anger in 21:1-14. At the same time, the last sentence of 24:25 creates a link back to the final words of 21:14 ("heeded supplications for the land"). These two narratives turn out to be more or less similar. Both speak of an affront to the Lord leading to a disaster that the king successfully seeks to avert. These similarities have been strengthened by the work of the redactor who brought together various earlier materials to create 2 Samuel 21–24. This redactor has constructed chapters 21–24 into a conclusion for the book of Samuel by fashioning the material into a pleasing concentric pattern:

A: famine story (21:1-14)
B: warriors (21:15-22)
C: psalm (22:1-51)
C': poem (23:1-7)
B': warriors (23:8-39)
A':plague story (24:1-25)

This section appears to have been purposely edited to fit its present location. The story of 2 Samuel 21:1-14 looks back to Saul and his failures, while 24:1-15 can be understood as pointing forward to the temple that Solomon will soon build in Jerusalem. Other more subtle editorial connections emerge upon closer inspection. The solidarity issue referred to in 24:17 is previewed in 23:13-17, and David's trusting piety of 24:14 echoes the poetry of 22:7. This section interrupts the story of the succession to David's throne at the end of 2 Samuel 20. The theme of succession does not pick up again until 1 Kings 1. David is still in his full vigor, in marked contrast to 1 Kings 1:1-4. Thus, a redactor has constructed these four chapters out of earlier materials in order to conclude Samuel and to signal the division of Samuel from Kings. This conclusion describes the high point of David's military prowess and faithful piety.

The later retelling of this story in 1 Chronicles 21 provides the interpreter with another instructive example of redaction. In this case, the redaction critic has the unusual luxury of comparing the original text and the redacted text. Reading Samuel and Chronicles side-by-side is a useful exercise in learning how to do redaction criticism. The practice of editorial modification is immediately apparent when 2 Samuel 24:1 is compared with

1 Chronicles 21:1. The author of Chronicles attributes the incitement of the census to Satan rather than to the Lord. This modification was motivated by changes in theology about the nature of God and the origin of moral evil in the world. In the time between the composition of 2 Samuel 24 and the work of the Chronicler, the figure of Satan (the Accuser) had emerged as a buffer between the direct action of God and supernatural tests and temptations (compare Job 1–2).

The Chronicler as redactor also safeguards propriety involving the Levites (1 Chr 21:6) and enhances the glory of the future Temple site (the higher price of v. 25; cf. 2 Sam 24:24). Another noticeable editorial change is the portrayal of Ornan (= Araunah) and his four sons as supplementary witnesses to the angel's appearance (1 Chr 21:20). The Chronicler also makes it completely clear that the threshing floor was precisely the site of Solomon's Temple (1 Chr 22:1).[8]

READING FOR HISTORICAL DEVELOPMENT (HISTORICAL CRITICISM)

Most biblical texts are composite productions that developed in stages. This concept of literature produced corporately by members of a culture over generations is contrary to modern notions of authorship. Such literature is a cultural artifact rather than the product of an individual. Until they became fixed by increasing respect for their integrity and eventual canonization, biblical texts changed over time. Those who copied and used them tended to expand, revise, and reinterpret them. A careful comparison of parallel versions of the same text demonstrates this process at work. It is instructive to compare Exodus 20:1-17 and Deuteronomy 5:6-21; Joshua 15:13-19 and Judges 1:10-15; Joshua 21:4-42 and 1 Chronicles 6:54-81; or Psalms 14 and 53. The careful reader can often detect earlier forms of a text behind or underneath its present configuration. This activity is called historical criticism. Historical criticism seeks to uncover the history of a text's development over time. It seeks to answer questions such as: By what path did the text reach its present shape? Can we trace earlier stages in its development? What previously independent texts or sources were utilized? For whom and in what circumstances was the text created? What cultural and historical situations are reflected in the various stages of the text's evolution?

A careful reading of 2 Samuel 24 uncovers difficulties in the flow of the narrative that point to the development of the narrative over time. Is the reason for the plague the Lord's anger or David's sin? Why does David repent before Gad offers the three choices and before punishment can begin? Does the plague stop because it is "the appointed time" (v. 15) or because the Lord relents and commands the angel (v. 16)? Alternatively, does it continue (v. 17) so that it stops only at verse 25? Is David's act of altar building prompted by his vision at Araunah's threshing floor (v. 16) or by Gad's recommendation (vv. 18-19)? Although some of these irregularities function to create certain literary effects in the present form of the story, their actual origin is best explained by the assumption that the text developed over successive generations.

Investigating the compositional history of a text is not done merely for reasons of arcane historical interest, but because it provides another perspective for reading and interpretation. Reading the later parts of a text over against the older portions lets each perspective stand out more clearly. By separating them chronologically, the individual voices of what may seem to be an untidy muddle are given a chance to speak out more clearly. Unfortunately, many readers find the task of using historical criticism frustrating. When seeking out guidance from introductions and commentaries, they quickly discover that scholars tend to disagree about all but the most obvious conclusions about what is early and late in a given text.

For example, there have been two basic approaches to the historical criticism of 2 Samuel 24. One suggests that an older, foundational account was expanded and supplemented by later interests. However, there has been little agreement about the content of the original text. The second approach has been to postulate that three originally independent narratives have been joined together: a census story (vv. 1-10), a plague story (vv. 11-15), and an altar-building story (vv. 16-25). The problem with this proposal is that the census episode needs the resulting plague to give it a narrative point, while the altar story needs the plague to provide its motivation.[9] The approach taken here proposes that two independent narratives have been merged, rather than three.

In its present form, the three movements of the story (census, 2 Sam 24:1-10; plague, vv. 11-15; and altar building, vv. 16-25) are tightly linked to one another. The census motivates the punishment, which in turn motivates the construction of the altar. The figure of the angel holds the plague and altar episodes together and leads to a reference back to David's sin in taking a census (vv. 16-17). However, the word used in verses 13 and 15 (NRSV: pestilence) is different from that used in verses 21 and 25 (NRSV: plague). This appears to be evidence that the text has not always been a unified whole. It is possible that the "census plus pestilence" plot (vv. 1-15 and parts of vv. 16-17) was once narrated alone as an illustration of sin, repentance, and God's mercy. It is also possible that an independent "plague plus altar" story line (parts of vv. 16-17 and vv. 18-25) could have functioned to legitimate the Jerusalem altar and tell the story of its foundation. These two originally independent stories were later brought together, cemented into a single plot by the shared theme of pestilence-plague and the figure of the angel taken from the altar-building story. This reconstruction is admittedly conjectural, but at least such an attempt at historical criticism lets the interpreter isolate some of the text's perspectives from others.

Observations about 2 Samuel 24:5-7 are less speculative. Form criticism suggests that what was once a boundary description has been turned into an itinerary (see foregoing discussion). Joab's route is missing from the Chronicler's retelling and thus was probably not yet part of the version of Samuel used by that author. The focus of this route is on lost territory east of the Jordan and in the north. It exhibits a typically postexilic concern to lay claim to ancestral land lost over the course of the centuries. For these reasons, it is likely that verses 5-7 represent a perspective later than the rest of the chapter. The status of this section as a later addition does not mean the interpreter should ignore it or discount it, however. Instead, it should be permitted to speak with its own distinctive voice as part of the whole text.

In conclusion, historical criticism suggests that there are at least three different viewpoints in 2 Samuel chapter 24 arising from differing historical and theological perspectives.

• One part of the text (the "census plus pestilence plot") declares that divine favor results from God's unmotivated mercy coupled with human repentance. It presents David as a fallible king who nonetheless is faithful to the Lord. This viewpoint offers support for the Davidic monarchy, while warning that unrestrained royal power can lead to national catastrophe. It seems reasonable to date these concerns generally to the monarchy period.

• Another voice (the "plague plus altar plot") insists that the effectiveness of ritual and sacrifice must not be ignored. It supports the royal altar at the Jerusalem Temple as an authentic and effective place of sacrifice. It counters negative reactions to the notion of building an altar and sacrificing to Israel's God in a pagan city on an alien spot widely known as "the threshing floor of Araunah the Jebusite." This viewpoint stresses that Jerusalem has a special status in God's eyes. This level of the narrative seems to come from relatively early in the monarchy period, arising in a time when concerns over Jerusalem's foreign past would still have been troubling to some.

• A third voice, the itinerary of verses 5-7, reflects a longing that Israel might someday regain land lost after defeat and exile. This concern would most likely have surfaced in the postexilic period.

READING AS CANON (CANONICAL CRITICISM)

This narrative and the book that contains it have been the focus of such intense interpretative efforts because they are part of a canon of scripture. As canon, the story of David's census is part of a larger whole and is in some sense authoritative or normative for the faith communities of Judaism and Christianity. Canonical criticism sets aside questions about a text's historical development. Instead, it asks how the final form of a text relates to that larger canon of which it is a part.

Setting a text into its canonical context can generate fields of meaning that go beyond anything present in the minds of the original writers and readers. For example, Jerusalem and David are enormously significant objects of faith in the canon of scripture. Therefore, the special status of Jerusalem and its altar promoted in 2 Samuel 24 resonates with texts as diverse as Zion psalms such as Psalm 46 and eschatological promises like Zechariah 14:16-21. Similarly, David's role here as repentant sinner can be read against the background of other stories of his failures and fidelity. It also provides a commentary on God's promise of an eternal Davidic dynasty because of David's obedience (1 Kgs 15:4-5). Moreover, as the concluding episode of the book of Samuel, this chapter serves as a canonical commentary on all that has been reported about David and a guide for how the various stories about David ought to be read. David is a model of repentant faith, and his accomplishments are the result of God's mercy and purpose.

The most overarching issue in the canon of scripture has to do with God's nature and God's way of relating to humanity. This story reveals the character of Israel's God as one who incites David, gives him a choice of punishments, but then "relented concerning the evil" (2 Sam 24:16). It suggests that God's rich gifts are not to be anxiously counted up or seen as tokens of pride. They cannot be enumerated in an attempt to secure them or hold on to them, and to try to do so can lead to catastrophe. Moreover, in this story God remains hidden and fearfully awesome, acting out of unexplained anger and provoking David into sin (v. 1). Yet, the final outcome shows that David's choice to "fall into the hand of the LORD, for his mercy is great" (v. 14) was indeed the only correct one. Canonically, this story may be seen as a narrative illustration of the classic and often repeated description of the Lord as "merciful and gracious, slow to anger, and abounding in steadfast love and faithfulness" (Exod 34:6; Num 14:8; etc.).

PART TWO

READING THROUGH ISRAEL'S HISTORICAL STORY

CHAPTER 4

DEUTERONOMISTIC HISTORY AND CHRONISTIC BOOKS

THE DEUTERONOMISTIC HISTORY

Many Old Testament scholars believe that a single author or editor assembled most of the material in Joshua, Judges, Samuel, and Kings. This writer is customarily labeled the Deuteronomistic Historian (abbreviated DH or Dtr). This Deuteronomistic Historian was an editor who assembled together items of older material from Israel's scribal tradition. However, DH was not just a collector, but also a creative *author* who organized this large aggregate of data into a coherent whole and gave it a distinctive theological outlook. As one who recounted past events systematically, while tracing the interplay of cause and effect, DH fully deserves the title of historian. As a historiographer, DH's goal was to explain the meaning and significance of the past for a contemporary readership (see chapter 1).[1]

DH begins this history by incorporating the existing book of

Deuteronomy and furnishing it with an enclosing framework (Deuteronomy 1–3, 31, 34). In addition, the final form of DH consists roughly of Joshua 1–12, 23; Judges 2–16; 1 Samuel 1 through 2 Samuel 20; and all of 1 and 2 Kings.[2] DH tells the story of Israel in the land, beginning from the conquest of Canaan and climaxing with the reform of Josiah king of Judah (2 Kings 22–23). The present form of DH continues the story to the early exile. The central interpretative theme is that Israel's fate in the land hinged on the nation's obedience or disobedience to the law of Moses as set forth in the book of Deuteronomy.

The final form of DH clearly dates from the early exile and reports on events up to the death of Judah's last king (2 Kgs 25:30; sometime after 560 BCE). The purpose of DH in its final form was to explain the overthrow of the nation as a justified divine punishment for the religious misdeeds of the people and their kings. The overall outlook is pessimistic. It remains unclear how much if any hope this final writer had for the disobedient nation's future. On the one hand, Israel's repentance in the book of Judges led repeatedly to the Lord's forgiveness. Yet the final paragraph of DH, which records the release of the last scion of the Davidic kingship (2 Kgs 25:27-30) is completely ambiguous. Is the report of the release of King Jehoiachin intended to foreshadow a hopeful future for Judah? Or does it mark the end of all hopes for a renewal of the Davidic dynasty? Solomon's prayer dedicating the Temple speaks of prayers offered up in distant exile (1 Kgs 8:46-51). However, it does not venture to hope for a return for the exiles, only a more bearable life in the land of their captors (v. 50).

However, scholars disagree about whether this largely pessimistic exilic configuration was actually the first form in which DH appeared. Many have suggested that the original Deuteronomistic Historian wrote a generation earlier, during or just after the reign of Josiah (d. 609 BCE). The chief evidence for this is a perplexing tension within DH between two main theological themes, one optimistic and the other largely pessimistic. Overall, the final exilic form of DH has a negative attitude about the institution of kingship. The ultimate destruction of Judah is predicted early in the history of the monarchy (e.g., 1 Kgs 9:6-9). Particular blame is directed at King Manasseh, whose religious apostasy is described in 2 Kings 21:10-15 as the decisive cause of Judah's fall.

In contrast, much of DH strongly expresses a contradictory and distinctly more optimistic theme. Of course the institution of kingship leads to transgression, especially "the way of Jeroboam son of Nebat, who caused Israel to sin" by establishing illegitimate worship at Bethel (1 Kgs 22:52; cf. 1 Kgs 15:26, 34, etc.). Yet time after time the nation's repentance leads to forgiveness from the Lord and restoration. The pattern of apostasy followed by punishment, repentance, and deliverance is expressed both in the structure of the book of Judges and in Solomon's dedicatory prayer of 1 Kings 8. Solomon's prayer emphasizes the theme of returning to the Lord in repentance (vv. 33, 35, etc.). A second element in this more positive outlook is the essential role played by the family of David in the nation's life before God. The Lord's extraordinary promise of a perpetual dynasty to David, first made in the oracle of Nathan (2 Sam 7:1-17), is repeated over and over (e.g., 1 Kgs 11:36; 15:4; 2 Kgs 8:19).[3]

The high point of this positive thematic trajectory is the reformation of Josiah reported in 2 Kings 22–23. At this turning point, the themes of obedient return to the Lord and the special significance of the Davidic family both reach their climax. Josiah applies the commandments of Deuteronomy to Judah's corporate life. In obedience to Deuteronomy 12, he removes the high places (open-air sanctuaries for sacrifice) that DH repeatedly condemns as sinful and undoes the dreadful transgression of Jeroboam by closing down the sacrificial center at Bethel.

Thus, there is a distinct contrast between the optimistic themes of God's promise to David and the effectiveness of repentance and the pessimistic theme of punishment for the nation's incessant transgression. This antithesis indicates to many interpreters that DH was originally a preexilic work written under the influence of the optimism generated by Josiah's reformation. Perhaps it was written before his death or finished just after it as a way of advocating the continuation of his policies.

DH incorporated various earlier sources to write this history. Especially in Joshua and Samuel, DH used these older sources without making significant changes. Most of these sources have been uncovered through the methods of historical criticism (see chapter 3), although DH also explicitly names three sources used in Kings (1 Kgs 11:41; 14:19, 29). For Joshua, DH adapted an earlier collection of conquest stories (Joshua 2–11). Chapter

7 of this volume will treat three of DH's sources in the book of Samuel: the Ark Story, the Rise of David, and the Throne Succession Story. A number of stories about the prophets were used to compose Kings (e.g., in 1 Kings 11, 13, 14, 20, 22; 2 Kings 9–10, 13, 18–20). DH also incorporated an established cycle of tales about the prophets Elijah and Elisha (in 1 Kings 17–19, 21; 2 Kings 1–8).[4]

UNIFYING TECHNIQUES IN DH

In bringing together such a wide variety of sources with differing viewpoints, DH faced a great challenge as an author. On the one hand, DH generally left these disparate sources unchanged and in large measure permitted them to speak for themselves. Yet, DH also wanted to use them to support theological themes derived from Deuteronomy and needed to impose a degree of unity and structure on them. Consequently, DH employed both structural and thematic means to unify this sprawling work.

One important unifying technique was the use of chronology. In fact, DH uses two unifying chronological systems that partially overlap. For the first part of the work (Deuteronomy through 1 Kings 8), DH counts a 480-year chronology reaching from the exodus from Egypt to the building of Solomon's temple (Solomon's fourth year; 1 Kgs 6:1). The heart of this system is found in the book of Judges. For each of the judges DH gives a time of oppression by one of Israel's enemies (for example, eighteen years serving Eglon; Judg 3:14). This is followed by a period of "rest" brought on by the victories of the judge (eighty years after Ehud; Judg 3:30).[5] Other passages give time spans for the career of Moses after the Exodus (Deut 1:3) and the periods of Joshua (five years; Josh 14:10), Saul (1 Sam 13:1), and David (1 Kgs 2:11). Although the figures no longer come out exactly right because of some later addition or disturbance in the text, in their original form they added up to 480 years and were clearly intended to provide a unifying focus. DH employed a second chronology based on the reigns of the kings of Israel and Judah. This system begins with the reign of Saul (1 Sam 13:1) and David (2 Sam 5:4-5). It continues in the book of Kings from Solomon (1 Kgs 11:42) down to the end of Judah's independence (2 Kgs 24:18).

70

These chronological frameworks provide DH with structure, unity, and a sense of historical breadth and credibility. The overlap of these two systems on Solomon points to the construction of the Temple and the reign of Solomon as pivotal events in Israel's history. The accession of Solomon was the first fulfillment of God's promise to David (2 Samuel 7), and construction of the temple meant that Deuteronomy's demand for centralized sacrifice (Deuteronomy 12) could now be applied (contrast 1 Kgs 3:2). Yet Solomon's reign also inaugurated a new stage of transgression, for the principle of centralized sacrifice was violated by the kings that followed him, both in Judah and in the Northern Kingdom of Israel. Most of these kings, beginning with Solomon himself (1 Kgs 11:1-13), led the people into religious apostasy.

A second structural technique used by DH is a framework of prophecy and fulfillment pairs. A prophet announces an upcoming event and then this forecast is fulfilled at a later point in the history. The most striking of these pairs constructs a bridge between 1 Kings 13 and 2 Kings 23. A prophet announces that someday a future king of the house of David will desecrate and demolish the renegade altar just built and dedicated by King Jeroboam of Israel. The prophet even predicts that this reforming king's name will be Josiah (1 Kgs 13:2-3). Thirty-two chapters and about three hundred years later, DH returns to this word and declares that it was fulfilled in the policies of Judah's reforming king Josiah (2 Kgs 23:16-18). The fulfillment of prophetic word demonstrates that the events of history are driven by God's will and that the word that God gives prophets to speak is to be trusted. Other examples of prophecy and fulfillment pairs are:

• A curse on Jericho is pronounced and executed (Josh 6:26 and 1 Kgs 16:34).
• A new priestly family replaces that of Eli (1 Sam 2:27-36 and 1 Kgs 2:27).
• David's son builds the Temple (2 Sam 7:13 and 1 Kgs 8:20).
• The kingdom is divided and part given to Jeroboam (1 Kgs 11:29-31 and 1 Kgs 12:15).
• The ruling families of Jeroboam (1 Kgs 14:10-11 and 15:29), Baasha (1 Kgs 16:2-4 and 16:12), and Ahab (1 Kgs 21:21-24 and 22:38; 2 Kgs 9:7-10 and 9:36-37) are eliminated.

DH used a third system of organization to pull together the complex story of Israel's history in the land. There are reflective pauses in the action at critical turns in the narrative. A character such as Moses or Joshua or Samuel steps out to center stage and delivers a summarizing speech. DH composed these "end of era speeches" in order to summarize the events of history and to proclaim their significance in light of the author's theology. These speeches look back in time to explore meaning and then look forward to forecast the future in terms of God's promises and threats. In composing speeches for important characters, DH anticipated the practice of Thucydides (*Peloponnesian War* I.xxii.1). However, the literary composition of such speeches was also a feature of Mesopotamian historiography.[6]

One example is 1 Samuel 12. This is a speech put into the mouth of Samuel as the era of the judges ends and the era of kingship begins. Samuel reviews the Lord's saving deeds from the exodus through the period of the judges (vv. 7-11). Whenever Israel cried to the Lord in repentance, the Lord saved them. Now the Lord has replaced those judges with the king for which Israel has asked (Saul). If the people and their king are obedient, all will be well, but rebellion against the Lord will lead to disaster. By inserting this speech, DH signals a shift in eras from the cyclical period of the judges to the era of kingship, in which king and people stand together before God in obedience or disobedience. The other end-of-era speeches in DH are:

• Moses reviews history leading up to the conquest (Deuteronomy 1–3).
• The Lord promises Joshua a successful conquest if he will be courageous and obedient (Josh 1:1-9).
• Just before his death, Joshua warns Israel about the challenges that face them in their new land (Joshua 23).
• The prophet Nathan promises that the Lord will grant David a successor and a dynasty that will reign in Jerusalem always (2 Sam 7:5-16).
• At the dedication of the temple, Solomon prays about its future significance (1 Kgs 8:22-53).
• In the final form of the book, the voice of the author reviews the reasons for the fall of the Northern Kingdom and points out similarities to Judah's perilous situation (2 Kgs 17:7-41).

DH also presents summary commentaries (although not in speech form) in Joshua 12 (a list of conquered enemy kings) and Judges 2:11-23 (the cyclical pattern of the judges).

THEOLOGICAL THEMES IN DH

DH also achieves integration of the disparate materials it contains by a persistent repetition of theological themes. The most characteristic of these is a doctrine of divine punishment and reward derived from Deuteronomy. Apostasy and disloyalty to the Lord inevitably bring wrath and punishment, but return, repentance, and fidelity to the law written in Deuteronomy bring salvation and blessing (see, e.g., Judg 2:11-18; 1 Kgs 2:3-4; 8:33-34, 46-53; 2 Kgs 17:21-23).

According to DH, Israel transgressed against God by being disloyal in two fundamental ways. The first was the worship of "other gods" (Josh 23:16), that is, any god but Yahweh, Israel's national God. This was Israel's sin in the period of the judges (Judg 2:12, 17, 19; 1 Sam 8:8), but also during the monarchy (1 Kgs 11:4; 2 Kgs 22:17). DH points to the temptation of the local Canaanite Baal in the period of the judges (Judg 2:11, 13; 8:33; 10:6; 1 Sam 12:10). DH also condemns the worship of a foreign form of Baal sponsored by the family of Ahab in both the Northern Kingdom (1 Kgs 16:31-32; 18:18; 22:53) and in Judah (2 Kgs 8:18, 27). In regard to Judah, DH attacks a resurgence of Baal worship and the veneration of Assyrian deities ("the host of heaven") under King Manasseh (2 Kgs 21:3, 5). Israel's long history of disloyalty is concluded by Josiah's reformation, which abolished the worship of both Baal and the host of heaven (2 Kgs 23:4-5).[7]

The second heinous transgression was to sacrifice to the Lord at any site other than Jerusalem. Deuteronomy chapter 12 insists that Israel's only altar of sacrifice was to be at a single, central sanctuary, "the place that the LORD your God will choose . . . to put his name there" (v. 5). Although Deuteronomy never identifies this place, in DH the Lord expressly chooses Jerusalem as the location for the central temple (2 Samuel 7, 1 Kings 8). DH particularly condemns sacrifice by the kings of the Northern Kingdom at Bethel. This holy place was a national shrine founded by Israel's first king, Jeroboam, along with one at the city of Dan (1 Kgs 12:26-33). Sacrifice at the shrine of Bethel was doubly offensive to DH because the Lord was worshiped there in the form of an idol. This image of Israel's God, contemptuously referred to as a "golden calf," represented divine power in the form of a bull. Without exception, DH judges each of the kings of the Northern Kingdom as wicked because they continued this practice, "walking in the way of Jeroboam" (1 Kgs 15:26, 34, etc.). In Judah, noncentral sacrifice was practiced at high places, local open-air altars. DH criticizes many of the kings of Judah for permitting sacrifice outside Jerusalem at these provincial shrines. Only Hezekiah and especially Josiah promoted exclusive sacrifice at Jerusalem as national policy. Hezekiah therefore receives unqualified approval from DH (2 Kgs 18:3-6). DH praises Josiah as David's equal in faithfulness because his reformation went even further, closing down the high places (2 Kgs 23:8-9, 19-20) in the territory of both kingdoms and desecrating Jeroboam's detestable shrine of Bethel (vv. 15-18).

Although punishment for apostasy and blessings for fidelity permeate DH as its main theological theme, other theological principles are also advanced:

• The promised land is a wonderful gift from the Lord, but God might take it away (Josh 1:2-6; chap. 23).
• The Jerusalem temple is the place that the Lord is always available for prayer and worship (1 Kings 8).
• Because of David's exceptional obedience, the Lord promised that his family would rule in Jerusalem in perpetuity (1 Kgs 11:36; 15:4-5; 2 Kgs 8:19).
• Repeatedly, the Lord has warned king and nation through the words of the prophets. DH could be characterized as a history of the prophetic word of promise and threat at work in the life of Israel.
• Josiah is the hero of DH. His reform marks the high point of loyalty to God and obedience to the law. In many ways, Joshua serves as a prototype for Josiah, and King Hezekiah functions as his forerunner.
• In the final form of DH, the infamous sins of King Manasseh of Judah overshadow the virtues of his grandson Josiah. Judah's final defeat at the hands of the Assyrians was the consequence of an apostasy the Lord could no longer forgive (2 Kgs 21:10-15; 22:16-17; 24:3-4).

THE PLOT OF DH

As one would expect from a historiographic composition, the plot of DH focuses on cause and effect in order to reveal the meaning of past events (see chapter 1). The warnings of Moses (Deuteronomy 31) and Joshua (Joshua 23) set up the central problem of the plot. Will Israel continue in obedience to the law of Moses and prosper, or will the people disobey and suffer the Lord's wrath? The story begins on a hopeful note. Moses transfers his authority to Joshua, who leads Israel in a unified and wholly successful invasion of the land of promise (Joshua 1–12). After Joshua's death, however, optimism fades. Israel abandons its former obedience and begins to worship other gods (Judges 2). The Lord punishes this disloyalty by letting enemies dominate them, but repeatedly Israel turns back in repentance to exclusive worship of the Lord. Each time their penitence persuades the Lord to send military leaders (judges) to deliver them (Judges 3–16; 1 Samuel 1–7).

The plot takes a new twist and breaks out of this incessant cycle of apostasy and return when the people demand a king to rule over them (1 Samuel 8). The Lord reluctantly acquiesces to this new pattern and helps them choose Saul (1 Samuel 9–12). Saul starts off well (1 Samuel 13–14), but quickly proves to be disobedient (1 Samuel 15). In contrast, his successor David is nearly perfect in his obedience. As a result, the Lord rewards David with an astounding promise. His son will build the single central sanctuary called for in Deuteronomy. Moreover, the Davidic dynasty will rule perpetually in Jerusalem (2 Samuel 7).

David's son Solomon brings both these promises into effect. It seems finally as though Israel will reach the goal of faithful obedience to Deuteronomy and enjoy security and prosperity in the land. At first Solomon reigns in obedience and glory (1 Kings 3–10), but in his old age he strays into the worship of "other gods" (1 Kings 11). Israel is once more seduced into disobedience. In a sense, the plot movement is repeating itself. Initially the optimism of Joshua was followed by the stagnated pattern of Judges, in which disobedience and obedience alternated. Now the positive possibilities of David and Solomon have degenerated into a futile succession of kings, some of them loyal, but more of them disobedient. The twin blessings of Davidic kingship and central sanctuary have not yet reached their divinely intended potential. Consequently the narrative tension not only persists, but intensifies.

The punishment for Solomon's sin is a division of the kingdom, although Judah remains with David's family because of the Lord's promise. The northern kings immediately fall away into illegitimate worship at Bethel and Dan (1 Kings 12–13). At the instigation of the family of Ahab, they sin with other gods (1 Kings 16). Some of Judah's kings are obedient, in spite of the fact that they continued to permit sacrifice outside Jerusalem. Others commit serious apostasy. When the Lord finally destroys the Northern Kingdom because of its accumulated sins (2 Kings 17), the plot moves toward its climax. God's wrath and destruction threaten Judah as well. Will they turn and be saved, or continue to follow Israel's path to defeat and exile? As the moment of decision for Judah approaches, the gap between wicked and virtuous kings widens. They become more extreme examples of corruption or integrity. Hezekiah is as virtuous as David was (2 Kings 18–20), but Manasseh is the archetype of depravity (2 Kings 21).

King Josiah marks the decisive turning point in the plot of DH. The story reaches a positive climax when he enforces the reforms of Deuteronomy in Judah and closes down all the local shrines (2 Kings 22–23). Moreover, he expands his reforming activities into the former Northern Kingdom, destroying and desecrating the shrine of Bethel and the northern high places. The future looks hopeful and optimistic, an echo of the golden age of David and Solomon. Josiah has eliminated the nation's lethal sins of noncentral sacrifice and the worship of other gods. Even a reunification of Judah and Israel under the rule of David's descendants seems to be possible.

Unfortunately, things did not turn out as DH had expected. King Josiah's premature death appears to have undermined his reform, and the policies of his successors resulted in the destruction of Judah and Jerusalem by Babylon. As a result, a second, pessimistic plot was imposed over DH's originally optimistic one. In this plot, Israel's history in the land is one of disobedience from the very onset. Although the Lord incessantly warns them (Judg 2:1-5; 6:7-10; 1 Kgs 9:6-9), faithfully sending "his servants the prophets" (2 Kgs 17:13, 23; 21:10; 24:2), the nation continues to disobey. In the end, even the righteousness of Hezekiah and Josiah makes no difference. King Manasseh's wickedness is so appalling that the destruction of Judah becomes unavoidable (21:10-15; 24:3-4). Judah's future remains an open question. Perhaps there is a chance for a new start if their offspring in exile repent, perhaps not. It all depends on what the Lord chooses to do.

THE CHRONISTIC BOOKS

Some scholars have suggested that Chronicles and Ezra-Nehemiah once made up a single, unified work something like the Deuteronomistic History. Those who emphasize the similarities in style and outlook between Chronicles and Ezra-Nehemiah sometimes designate them as the Chronistic Work or the Chronicler's History.[8]

Chronicles is linked to Ezra and Nehemiah as a continuous story by the overlap of 2 Chronicles 36:22-23 and Ezra 1:1-3. Chronicles and Ezra-Nehemiah unquestionably display similarities in outlook, theme, and style. Both consider the practices and personnel of Jerusalem temple worship to be critical historical data. Both use the prayers of heroes of the faith to interpret events (2 Chr 20:5-12 and Ezra 9:6-15). In both works, the ideal goal for the community of Judah is to remain an obedient and holy people. The second-century Jewish book of 2 Esdras, which depends directly on 2 Chronicles 35–36, Ezra 1–10, and Nehemiah 8, also might be cited as evidence that these books once existed as a single work.

More recently, however, it has become common to point to indications that the two works developed separately as independent literary compositions. For example, Chronicles utilized Samuel and Kings as its chief source, but Ezra-Nehemiah depended on a large number of sources, including official documents, demographic lists, and biographical materials. There are indications that Ezra-Nehemiah was completed a generation before Chronicles was composed. The emphasis on the "doctrine of retribution," which is so prominent in Chronicles (see chapter 9), is essentially absent from Ezra-Nehemiah. Moreover, Chronicles has a positive and inviting attitude about the loyal citizens of the Northern Kingdom. This stands in sharp contrast to the hostile and exclusionary point of view about non-Judahites promoted in Ezra-Nehemiah.

Nevertheless, it seems clear that Chronicles and Ezra-Nehemiah address audiences who are in similar situations and reflect related, although not identical, theological perspectives. In order to capture both the similarities and differences between Chronicles and Ezra-Nehemiah, I have chosen to designate them as the Chronistic books.

This complex of books begins with genealogies, starting with Adam (1 Chr 1:1). The actual historical narrative starts with David (1 Chronicles 10). The story moves forward through his piety and glory (1 Chronicles 11–29) and that of his successor Solomon (2 Chronicles 1–9). After the division of the united kingdom, the narrative traces the ups and downs of the southern kingdom of Judah (2 Chronicles 10–35). Defeat and exile (2 Chronicles 36) are followed by a return from captivity and the reconstruction of the Jerusalem temple (Ezra 1–6). The Chronistic books conclude with the religious and social reformations of Ezra (Ezra 7–10, Nehemiah 8–10) and Nehemiah (Nehemiah 1–7, 11–13) in the period of the early Persian Empire.

The Chronistic books view God's people primarily as the religious community that worships at the Jerusalem temple. At first, this is David's united kingdom, then the kingdom of Judah, and finally the province of Judah in the Persian Empire.

CHAPTER 5

THE BOOK OF
JOSHUA

SHAPES AND STRUCTURES

Joshua divides in half rather neatly. Chapters 1–12 report military conquest, and 13–24 deal with settlement and life in the land. Alternatively, one may think of the book as divided into three acts: conquering the land (1–12), dividing the land (13–21), and warning about the future (22–24). The narrative portions of Joshua (1–11, 22–24) are the most interesting. They may be read straight through as a connected story that begins with the death of Moses and ends with the death of Joshua.

The reader should look for interconnections between the individual stories. The story of Rahab (chapter 2) leads to the conquest of Jericho (6), which leads in turn to the transgression of Achan (7). The defeat that results from Achan's sin moves into the capture of Ai (8). At the same time, the crossing of the Jordan (4–5) is linked to Jericho (6) by the notion of the ark in procession. The trick of the Gibeonites (9) and the enemy coalition led by the king of Jerusalem (10) both relate back to Israel's earlier successes at Jericho and Ai. News of Israel's success also inspires a coalition led by the king of Hazor in Joshua 11.

Joshua is a typical product of Israel's scribal tradition of reusing the literary legacy of previous generations to meet the needs of new audiences. The individual stories in Joshua began as oral folktales about local victories tied to local places such as city ruins (Josh 6:26; 8:28) or commemorative markers (4:20; 7:26). Later these tales were written down and gathered into a connected narrative as the triumphs of a unified Israel (Joshua 2–11). Later still, this collection of conquest stories was re-edited (growing to 1–12, 23) to form part of the Deuteronomistic History. This was a history of Israel in the land told from the perspective of Deuteronomy's theology (see chapter 4).

By ancient standards, DH was enormously long for a single work (Deuteronomy, Joshua, Judges, 1 and 2 Samuel, 1 and 2 Kings). A book was normally what would fit onto a single scroll of handy size. Consequently, DH was broken up into five individual books, each of which then experienced its own history of revision, updating, and growth. Deuteronomy (the story up to the death of Moses) was combined with Genesis, Exodus, Leviticus, and Numbers to become the Torah or Pentateuch, the core of the Hebrew canon. Likewise, the portion of DH that dealt with the career of Joshua, from "after the death of Moses" (Josh 1:1) to the death of Joshua (24:29-31), achieved its own independence as an individual book. It was probably only after this separation from DH that supplementary materials were added to Joshua to produce the book as it now stands in the canon. This added information includes the geographical data of Joshua 13–21, the controversy story of Joshua 22, and Joshua's final address in chapter 24.

Joshua consists of three types of material: speeches, narratives, and geographic descriptions. Theological addresses by the Lord and by Joshua constitute the book's introduction (chapter 1) and two conclusions (23–24). Narratives of conquest under the leadership of the Lord, who fought for Israel as a warrior, make up Joshua 2–11. Another narrative reports a controversy among the tribes about loyalty to the Lord and national unity (22). Chapters 12–21 consist of geography summarizing the conquest and describing the allocations to the twelve tribes in the form of city lists and boundary descriptions. Narrative, geography, and address all claim the land of promise for Israel and sustain the national identity of Israel as God's special people.

It is a good idea to keep a map or Bible atlas open in order to follow the action. The geography of conquest falls into three campaigns: central (chapters 6–8), south (10), and north (11). You can also use a map to follow the geography of Joshua's allotment of the land. The land east of the Jordan is distributed first (13), then the land of the most important tribes (Judah, Ephraim, Manasseh; 15–17), and finally the territories of the other, less significant tribes (18–19).

ISSUES IN READING

Joshua can be a disturbing book. It speaks of brutal conquest, confiscating the land of an indigenous people, and acts of wholesale slaughter. Many readers squirm when reading Joshua. They naturally read it against the background of conquests made by European settlers and colonial invaders in the Americas, Africa, and Asia. They may recognize distasteful aspects of their own national stories of invasion, bloodshed, settlement, and ruthless conflict between intrusive invaders and native cultures. For this reason, the portrayal of Israel's wholesale destruction of the Canaanites strikes a little too close to home. Just as disturbing is the concept of a crusading, nationalistic God who fights wars for one ethnic group at the expense of another. The modern reader may be tempted to dismiss Joshua as nothing more than a theological justification for the forceful appropriation of land that rightfully belongs to other people.

However, Joshua becomes somewhat more palatable if the reader understands that its relationship to actual history is not direct. Joshua is describing an idealistic and theoretical picture of Israel's origin in Canaan, not factual history. This romanticized epic represents an illusory invasion, conquest, and land allotment done by an idealized Israel, a unified people neatly organized into twelve tribes. Israel follows the resolute and law-abiding leadership of Joshua, the successor of Moses authorized by God. With God's help, they succeed easily.

In actual historical fact, however, such an effortless conquest never took place, as the less optimistic reports of Judges 1 make clear. Israel's emergence in the land occurred over a long period, not in the lifetime of a single generation. Moreover, Israel never completely annihilated the Canaanites, who survived into the monarchy period (1 Kgs 9:20-21). In fact, archaeology indicates that Israel emerged from within the land of Canaan, rather than invading it from the outside (see chapter 2). The actual story was more one of peaceful pioneers settling in new territory than brutal invaders wresting away another people's homeland.

In fact, the book of Joshua actually appeared as a way of dealing with Israel's persistently weak and vulnerable position, not as a celebration of its imperialistic triumph and dominance. The communities who wrote and read Joshua were constantly threatened by the loss of their land or dispossessed exiles hoping for its return. Attack from outside and foreign oppression repeatedly endangered Israel's possession of the land. These threats came first from their local neighbors, such as Edom, Moab, and the Canaanite city-states. Later the successive world empires of Assyria, Babylon, and Persia menaced Israel with the loss of its independence and land. The collapse of the kingdom of Israel (722 BCE) disconnected everything north of the kingdom of Judah from native political control, and subsequent pressure from Assyria on Judah led to additional losses of land on the west. With the fall of Judah (586 BCE), Edomite incursions alienated large tracts to the south. In the Second Temple period, the province of Judah consisted of only a fragment of Israel's earlier ancestral territory.

In other words, it was usually Israel who played the role of an indigenous people menaced by politically and technically superior foes. It was Israel whose culture and religion were endangered by hostile outsiders and the alien groups with whom Israel shared the land. The book of Joshua was part of Israel's reaction to the danger posed by its enemies. Joshua evokes this continuing threat by describing enemy kings with iron chariots and cities with impregnable walls. Retelling stories of past heroes was one way of conceptualizing and strengthening Israel's title to its homeland. In this way, Joshua served generation after generation of readers as a claim on the endangered land that they believed God had promised them.

THE PLOT OF JOSHUA

The final, canonical form of Joshua offers readers a reasonably coherent plot. The book begins and ends with interpretative speeches (chapters 1 and 23–24), as well as with transitions of leadership from Moses to Joshua (1:1-2) and then from Joshua to succeeding generations (24:29-31). The plot divides into two large movements.

The first movement (chapters 2–12) is oriented toward action and mobility and tells of Israel's foundational triumphs. This initial plot moves from promise to fulfillment and flows from the introductory pledges made by God to Joshua in chapter 1. Israel's victories represent the accomplishment of God's promises: "Every place that the sole of your foot will tread upon I have given to you" and "no one shall be able to stand against you" (Josh 1:3, 5). These narratives are cemented together by the repeated theme that the enemy has heard about Israel's advance and is afraid (2:9-10; 5:1; 9:1-2; 10:1-2; 11:1). Israel's triumphant advance is organized geographically into central (chapters 6–8), southern (9–10), and northern (11) campaigns.

In addition, complex interconnections link together the individual stories.

• Rahab, who aids the spies sent to Jericho (2), and the story of crossing the Jordan (3–4) both connect to the annihilation of Jericho in chapter 6 (see 4:19; 6:17, 22-23, 25).
• Jericho in turn ties to Achan's sin of appropriating the booty of Jericho in chapter 7 (6:18; 7:1). The discovery and resolution of Achan's transgression leads to the conquest of Ai in chapter 8 (7:2-5, 10-12).
• The defeat of Ai leads to the trick of the Gibeonites in chapter 9 (9:3-4).
• The Ai and Gibeonite episodes taken together motivate an attack by a coalition of southern kings (9:1-2; 10:1).
• The defeat of the southern coalition then instigates a parallel coalition of northern kings (11:1).

Episodes of worship and acts of obedience to God's law punctuate this plot of successful military action, first at Gilgal (Josh 5:2-12) and then at Shechem (8:30-35). These interludes of conscientious obedience also flow out of God's words in chapter 1, for when promising success the Lord also required careful observance of the law (1:7-8). Chapter 12 ends this first narrative movement by summing up the results of military conquest. This topographic list of defeated kings emphasizes the scope of Israel's victory, while simultaneously pointing forward to a second, geographically oriented plot movement.

Chapters 13–21 represent a second narrative movement. Geographic catalogs are presented in a narrative framework describing land distribution. This second movement is more static than the first. It describes the shape of idealized tribal settlement patterns. Whereas the actions of the first plot are predominantly optimistic, the second section sometimes admits to shortfalls in Israel's realization of total conquest (for example, Josh 15:63 and 16:10). This second movement is enclosed in a rough way by a repeated reference to Joshua's old age (13:1; 23:1). The geographic material is also held together by the positive evaluative brackets of 11:23 and 21:43-45, which emphasize that the Lord kept all the promises made in chapter 1. Joshua's charge to and dismissal of the east Jordan tribes (1:12-18; 22:1-6) form an even wider set of brackets that enclose and hold together the first and second plot movements.

In the second plot movement, the captured land is divided among the tribes by means of the divinely authorized process of the sacred lot (Josh 14:2). The plot organization reflects both geography and the hierarchy in importance of the individual tribes. First comes a review of what Moses had done for the tribes settled east of the Jordan (chapter 13). Distribution to the highly significant three central tribes follows next (14–17). Then a survey commission records and partitions the rest of the land, and the lot is used to apportion relatively equal portions to the other, less significant tribes (18–19). Land distribution redirects reader interest into the future and toward issues of Israel's life in the land. This subject is pursued further by a description of the cities of refuge (20) and the Levitical cities (21). Other narratives about land allocation are interspersed into this second plot movement. These episodes describe keeping earlier promises to Caleb, Othniel, and the daughters of Zelophehad (14:6-15; 15:13-19; 17:3-6) and solving problems (extra land for Joseph in 17:14-18 and a grant to Joshua in 19:49-50).

The final three chapters (22–24) serve to direct the implications of the two plot movements of conquest and land distribution at the reader's own situation. They warn about future developments as a settled nation and urge obedience and loyalty. The story of the altar built by the east Jordan tribes (Josh 22:9-34) performs this task by using a narrative format, while chapters 23 and 24 take a sermonic approach. The altar narrative of chapter 22 explores questions raised by the tribal land allotments and the resulting dispersal of the people. It urges the preservation of national unity and loyalty to the single sanctuary of a single God. It also looks to the future by raising the specter of punishment for disobedience (vv. 20, 31). The book reaches its conclusion with Joshua's interpretation of the meaning of the conquest in chapter 23. This is followed by a second summary in chapter 24 that reflects on the implications of the entire tradition of God's election of Israel as found in Genesis through Joshua.

The overall move of the book of Joshua is from the optimism of total conquest to the pessimism of partial failure. The reader experiences the flavor of promises yet to be redeemed (Josh 13:6; 17:18; 23:5), short-circuited by Israel's inability or disobedience (15:63; 16:10; 17:12-13; 23:12-13). This movement to blighted hope is completed by the threats of the last two chapters. These two speeches by Joshua warn Israel of the danger of future disloyalty to God and the terrible potential repercussions of defeat and exile. The reader is struck by the sharp contrast between Israel's ringing pledges of loyalty (24:16-18, 21, 24) and Joshua's threat of a punishment that appears to be nearly inevitable (23:15-16; 24:19-20). The unfolding future threatens a reversal of the gracious gift just bestowed in the conquest (23:12-13) and indeed a reversal of all God's saving acts (24:2-13). Joshua dies, and the future looks bleak. This prepares the reader for what is to follow in Judges and Kings.

CONTEXTS AND AUDIENCES

Like the other historical books, Joshua is the result of a writing process that took place over an extended period and involved the participation of a number of collectors, authors, and editors. Successive forms of Joshua were addressed to differing audiences at different periods and spoke to their particular contexts and conditions of life. The successive forms of Joshua imply at least three distinct sorts of readers over time.

The readers of Joshua's initial form (chapters 2–11) were concerned about national identity and their claim to the land of

Canaan. The reaction of the enemy unifies and organizes this earliest configuration of Joshua. They hear about Israel's exploits, they are afraid, and they react. This pattern is first set out by Rahab (Josh 2:9-11, 24), then repeated in 5:1 with reference to all enemy kings. Enemy reaction brackets the fall of Jericho in 6:1 and 27. Then in 9:1-4, enemy fear motivates both a hostile alliance and the Gibeonite trick. Finally it provokes coalition attacks in 10:1-5 and 11:1-5. The themes of external menace and internal national unity would have been important during the monarchy, when Israel's homeland was constantly under threat. Because the Lord as divine warrior gave their ancestors complete victory, these readers could be certain that the land of Canaan belonged to them. What they read in Joshua provided them with a sense of national unity, for the conquest was a cooperative project of "all Israel" (3:17; 8:15; etc.). This audience would also acquire explanations for the circumstances of their contemporary life in the land. What is the origin of those city ruins that dominate our landscape? Why do the descendants of Rahab and the Gibeonites continue to remain as independent ethnic communities within our borders?

The expanded form of Joshua that was part of the Deuteronomistic History (chapters 1–12, 23) was directed at a later audience concerned with the question of obedience to God's law. Israel's long, sad record of disobedience meant that God's threat of exile and defeat hung over these readers (Josh 23:14-16). For them, Joshua served as a challenge to follow the law of Moses as found in Deuteronomy (Josh 23:6-13). These readers learned that the fate of the nation depended on obedience and loyalty to God and the rejection of improper or pagan worship practices. Their ancestors' success in the conquest was a direct result of their obedience to Joshua, the authorized successor of Moses (1:1-9). The book seeks to convince these readers that careful obedience to the law of Deuteronomy (as in 8:30-35) would lead to total success (12:1-24) and the fulfillment of all God's promises (21:43-45). Elements of the native population that showed prudence (the Gibeonites) or faith (Rahab) survived the debacle. In contrast, those in Israel such as Achan who did not obey God's law were destroyed. Readers are told that they can visit the memorial stones at Gilgal. These witness to the wonders of God's past saving deeds and summon Israel to obedience

(4:6-7, 20-24). Israel's reward for careful observance of the law will be "rest from war" (11:23) and "rest . . . from all their enemies" (23:1); that is, the good fortune to enjoy God's gift of land in complete security.

The audience of the final form of Joshua was looking back to a glorious past and hoping for a better future. This audience appears to match the situation of Jews of the exile or of the Persian period. The outcome of Israel's chronic disobedience had been defeat, exile, and loss of national independence. However, these readers continued to dream of a return to a situation where everything would be restored to the way things were when Joshua and the high priest Eleazar were co-leaders (Josh 14:1; 19:51; 21:1). Nehemiah 8:17 witnesses to just such an aspiration.

Joshua presents these exilic and postexilic readers with a glorious vision of the golden past as a reflection of what they hope might be true again. The community is offered hope for a restoration of what has been lost and given a sense of connection with their pioneer ancestors who experienced God's mighty deeds. Israel possesses all its land again, town by town, border by border, tribe by tribe (chaps. 13–19). Defunct royal administrative systems (Josh 15:20-62; 18:21-28) are read back into the canonical past of Israel's origins. Each tribe has a place in the body politic, even those long vanished from the scene. The cities of refuge (20) and a nationwide presence of the Levites (21) are also part of this vision of an obedient, restored Israel. The story told in chapter 22 urges on readers the ideal of group unity and orthodoxy in worship at a single legitimate altar under priestly supervision. A long retrospective catalog of God's saving acts urges readers to place their ultimate choice in God once more (24).

The book of Joshua is a witness to the power of a shared story to generate, define, and defend the identity of a community. It is a literary production designed to create and support the identity of the people it repeatedly calls "all Israel" (Josh 3:17; 8:15; etc.). The book seeks to give its readers the courage to meet whatever present challenges face them because of their identity as the Lord's people. It also seeks to communicate hope for a future fulfillment of God's promises.

Readers are to understand themselves as the people of the Lord, the victorious divine warrior. As such, they are the rightful masters of the land of Canaan, whatever the present political situation may be. Israel's conscious self-identity is built by retelling the nation's past victories. Stories once told in different places by different segments of the population have been retold as the common achievements of "all Israel" under the common command of one leader (Josh 1:17; 3:7; 4:14; 6:27) at one time (10:42). The book uses another effective tactic to create internal unity when it sharply distinguishes between "us" ("all Israel") and "them" (the enemy Canaanites). Other techniques used to build national unity are the verbal maps of territory still claimed even after it had been lost to others and the evocation of the bygone twelve-tribe system.

Moreover, readers are encouraged to form themselves into an obedient people shaped by the demands of the law given through Moses. The Lord commanded Joshua not only to fight, but also to obey (Josh 1:7-8). Compliance with the law and the Lord's commands is a constant theme of the book of Joshua. It presents its readers with encouraging exhortations urging compliance with the law (chaps. 1, 23–24) and stories describing the rewards of obedience and the consequences of disobedience (7–8, 22). More specifically, readers are encouraged to observe circumcision and Passover in the proper manner (5:2-12). By building the altar at Shechem (8:30-35), Joshua carefully follows the directives of Deuteronomy 11:29-30 and 27:1-13. His public written display of the law there emphasizes its vital importance. His solemn reading of the law imposes the demand for obedience on the entire social structure of Israel, and on the reader as well.

Yet if much of the book asserts Israel's obedience, the issue of disobedience is also explored in the narratives about Achan (chapter 7) and the altar of the east Jordan tribes (22). The two final addresses of Joshua challenge the Israel of the future, that is the readers of the book, to obey the most important mandate of all, to worship the Lord alone (Josh 23:6-8, 11, 16; 24:14, 23).

THEMES

Leadership

Joshua raises the issue of faithful leadership. The leadership of Joshua stretches out between the death of Moses and his own death. He begins as the successor and servant of Moses ("assistant," Josh 1:1), but at the end is called "servant of the LORD" (24:29) in his own right. Although he is from the tribe of Ephraim (19:49-50; 24:30), as leader he serves as a unifying element for a diverse nation. The name "Joshua" means savior. As Israel's leader he is presented as the ideal savior, who not only won battles and secured possession of the land, but was able to hold the people to perfect loyalty his whole life (24:31).

Joshua is the authentic successor to Moses (Josh 1:5; 3:7; 4:14), and he follows the pattern set by Moses in several ways. Joshua's encounter with the commander of the Lord's army echoes Moses' experience at the burning bush (5:13-15 and Exod 3:2-5). He repeats Moses' function as intercessor (Josh 7:6-9 and Deut 9:25-29) and duplicates the Red Sea crossing by leading Israel across the Jordan (Josh 4:23). He holds up his sword against the enemy the way Moses held up his arms (Josh 8:18 and Exod 17:11). Joshua also follows Moses in the role of conqueror and distributor of the land (cf. Josh 12:1-6 with vv. 7-24). However, Joshua does not take over Moses' office as lawgiver (with the possible exception of 24:25), but instead consistently points back to the law which Moses gave as the standard for national fidelity (1:7-8, 13; 4:10; 8:30-35; 11:12-15; 22:2; 23:6).

Joshua is also presented as a royal figure, one that particularly resembles the great reformer, King Josiah (2 Kings 22–23). This becomes evident when one compares God's charge to Joshua in Joshua 1:2-9 with what is expected of the king in Deuteronomy 17:18-20 and 1 Kings 2:1-5. Like King Josiah he practices undeviating obedience to the law (Josh 1:7; 2 Kgs 22:2) and consequently can demand the same standard of others (Josh 23:6). Like Josiah he celebrates a proper Passover (Josh 5:10-12; 2 Kgs 23:21-23) and restructures a covenant of loyalty with God (Josh 8:30-35; 2 Kgs 23:2-3). Joshua thus serves as a forerunner and model for royal leadership, especially for the reforming policies of Josiah.[1]

The Land

The Lord's gift of the land is the central plot action of Joshua, constituting an arc of promise and fulfillment. The land was promised to Israel's ancestors and then to Joshua (Josh 1:2-6; 5:6), and God fulfilled this promise in the conquest (11:23; 21:43-45; 23:4-5; 24:13, 28). The concept of "rest" signifies Israel's confident possession of the land. Victory means that Israel has achieved this rest (1:13, 15; 21:44; 22:4; 23:1). A different Hebrew phrase, "the land had rest from war" (11:23; 14:15), communicates the peace experienced in the land after hostilities are over.

The importance of the promised land to Israel's sense of identity can hardly be overestimated.[2] Joshua repeatedly emphasizes that Canaan is a rich and good land (Josh 5:6, 12; 23:13, 15, 16). In the Hebrew Bible, land is not a mere commodity but an inheritance, passed down within the family by birthright. Because it was God's gift, one could not simply sell off family land in a commercial transaction. Joshua's use of the sacred lot to distribute the land (14:2; 19:51) communicates that God's authority stands behind Israel's settlement patterns. They were not the result of mere historical contingency. Because God as the divine warrior granted the land, Israel has an inalienable right to it, unless the Lord should choose otherwise (23:13, 15-16; 24:20).

Joshua is a book of mental maps. The dominant one is the territory of the twelve tribes, who completely fill up the land (Josh 13:7-33; 15:1–19:48). Two other, more expansive maps are also present. One is the "land that still remains" in 13:2-6, which consists of claimed but unconquered territory in Philistia and Phoenicia. The other is the expansionistic aspiration of Joshua 1:4, which conceives of the far-off Euphrates as the north boundary (cf. Deut 1:7; 11:24). These two utopian perspectives give a quality of unfulfilled promise to what Joshua says about the land. On the one hand, this shortfall is the result of Israel's disobedience or inability (15:63; 16:10; 17:12-13) and comes as a punishment from God (7:12; 23:12-13). However, this incompletely fulfilled promise also points to a hope for greater things to come (13:6; 17:18; 23:5). In Joshua, then, Israel's homeland represents both fulfilled promise and defaulted legacy. It is a token both of the Lord's power and fidelity and of Israel's faithlessness. It is the essence of Israel's national identity, simultaneously the object of hope and regret.

Most readers of Joshua soon notice an incongruity about Israel's occupation of the land. On the one hand, the conquest is asserted to be complete and the enemy nations entirely exterminated (Josh 1:3-6; 10:40-42; 11:16-23; 21:43-45). However, foreign peoples and unconquered land remain (13:2-6; 15:63; 16:10; 17:12-13; 23:4-5, 7, 12-13). Viewed historically, of course, this contradiction is the result of the book's growth and development over time. Yet, the reader of the final form of the book still needs to come to terms with this ambiguity. One way to do so is to think of alternative perspectives. The perspective of total and complete conquest celebrates God's power and integrity as one who keeps promises. At the same time, from the perspective of Israel's own efforts, the unfinished conquest is a sign of the nation's fallibility and disobedience to God's commands. Nevertheless, in the end, this paradoxical aspect of Joshua remains necessarily open-ended and enigmatic for the reader.

The Divine Warrior

Joshua understands ownership of the land in terms of conquest. As I have mentioned, the ideology of conquest was vital to Israel because their hold on the land was always tenuous. Consequently, these heartening conquest tales would have been important for readers in every generation. What is striking to modern readers is Israel's insistence that God fought directly for them and won these victories as the divine warrior. To extol one's god as a warrior was a common form of religious and political expression in the ancient Near East.[3] By recounting stories representing God as divine warrior, the book of Joshua praises God's power and graciousness. These divine warrior stories represent a theological confession, summarized in the creedlike statement "The LORD fought for Israel" (Josh 10:14, 42; 23:3, 10). The patterned repetition of victories in 10:28-39 and the methodical list of 12:9-24 are literary ways of suggesting the inevitability and totality of the divine warrior's victory. Ideologically the extermination of Canaan's traditional catalog of seven nations (3:10; 9:1; 11:3; 12:8; 24:11) glorifies the Lord as victorious warrior and promotes Israel's claim to the land.

What is most shocking to the modern reader is that the total enemy population is "devoted to destruction" (that is, set aside in a ceremonial way for destruction or slaughter). Examples of such wholesale destruction are recounted in Joshua 6:21; 8:26; 10:28-40; 11:11, 14. The idea behind this gruesome notion is that all property and people captured in these holy wars belonged completely to the Lord as the victorious divine warrior. Because it was the Lord's property, such booty could not be appropriated by humans or used for any human benefit. Therefore, all the spoils of war had to be either destroyed or given over to the temple treasury (6:19, 24). In a culture in which war captives automatically became the slaves of the victors, the enemy population in a war won by the divine warrior were to be killed in order to prevent their enslavement for human gain. Thus the complete slaughter of the enemy, so deeply offensive to the modern reader, is celebrated in Joshua as exemplary obedience to the commands of the Lord (10:40; 11:12, 15, 20).

CHAPTER 6

THE BOOK OF
JUDGES

SHAPES AND STRUCTURES

Judges continues Israel's story from the death of Joshua (Judg 1:1; 2:8) to just before the birth of Samuel. After an incomplete conquest that leaves much in the hands of their foes (chapter 1), Israel's life in the land falls into a drifting, recurrent pattern. Disloyalty leads to oppression by enemies, but when Israel cries out in repentance, the Lord sends deliverers (judges). Five of these judges are public military leaders (2–12). In contrast, Samson is a roguish hero who acts alone (13–16). In the last chapters (17–21), this cyclical pattern is replaced by a wholly negative account. A repeated pro-royalist refrain comments on Israel's depraved plunge into idolatry, violence, and civil war: "There was no king in Israel" (17:6; 18:1; 19:1; 21:25).

The repeated or cyclic pattern of Judges 2–16 is first outlined in 2:6-19. In contrast to the elders of Joshua's generation (2:7), a new generation unfamiliar with the Lord's saving acts sets this repeated pattern in motion (v. 10). First Israel would abandon the

Lord for other gods (vv. 11-13). This would lead to the Lord's anger and ensuing oppression by enemies (vv. 14-15). The Lord would then send judges to deliver Israel (vv. 16-18). However, the people would inevitably revert once more to the worship of other gods and begin the cycle again (v. 19).

The story of the first judge, Othniel, illustrates this pattern in a concise and prototypical fashion (Judg 3:7-10). The Othniel narrative adds a new item to the cycle. Israel's cry to the Lord (v. 9) appears as another stage, coming just before the rise of the deliverer. The Othniel story also adds a concluding notice that the "land had rest," that is, the people enjoyed an interval of peace (v. 11). The following Ehud story adds yet another item to the formula with the remark that the enemy was "subdued" (v. 30). All items of this pattern are present in the introductory and concluding formulas for Ehud, Deborah-Barak, and Gideon. The judges Othniel and Jephthah have less complete versions.[1] In contrast, Samson's story begins with Israel's apostasy and oppression by the Philistines (13:1), but the people do not cry out nor is the enemy subdued. Clearly with Samson, Israel's situation has changed for the worse.

The repeated cyclical pattern marshals these assorted stories into a theological argument about faithless disobedience and faithful and repentant obedience. Disloyalty to God leads to national catastrophe, but repentance and obedience can lead to deliverance. Yet Israel's proclivity for apostasy means that its history appears to be "stuck," going nowhere. If anything, Israel's behavior is actually getting worse and worse (Judg 2:19). In the end the last judge, Samson, fails to bring any meaningful deliverance whatsoever. Samson's failure points directly forward to the future successes of Samuel, who "judged Israel" (1 Sam 7:15) and by whom "the Philistines were subdued" (v. 13).

In addition to the six so-called major judges, Judges also preserves a concise list of others who "judged Israel" (Judg 10:1-5; 12:7-15). Family details glorify their wealth and eminence (10:4; 12:9, 14). These "minor judges" seem to have been civil officials rather than military leaders. Along with Tola, Jair, Ibzan, Elon, and Abdon, this older catalog also included Jephthah (12:7), so that he is both a major and a minor judge. The terms of service for the minor judges have been fitted into a larger chronology that also enumerates the years of each interval of enemy oppres-

94

sion and the ruling periods for each major judge. The uneven totals for the minor judges appear to be authentic (8, 10, 7, 6, 22, and 23 years). In contrast, the terms of the major judges are in schematic round figures (20, 40, or 80 years), suggesting that the editor who collected these stories concocted the figures.

The stories of the six major judges were originally independent tales of local heroes, but were collected together and fashioned into a succession of nationally important leaders, possibly in imitation of the list of minor judges. Because the minor judges "judged Israel," scholars conjecture that this was the source of the idea that the major judges also ruled over all Israel. This expression indicating nationwide leadership ("judged Israel") is used for both Othniel (Judg 3:10) and Samson (15:20; 16:21). The list of minor judges may also have provided the collector of these stories with the notion that the major judges served one after the other in an unbroken succession. It is historically more likely that they were local heroes whose influence was only regional and who partially overlapped in time. The circumstance that Jephthah was both a minor and a major judge probably contributed to these developments.

Evidence suggests that the cyclical pattern, the incorporation of the minor judges, the chronology, and the schematic story of Othniel, were all editorial contributions of the Deuteronomistic Historian (see chapter 4). Theological interests based on Deuteronomy are especially evident in Judges 2:1–3:6; 6:7-10; and 10:6-16.[2] Whether DH used an earlier collection of stories about deliverers is a matter of continuing debate.

Chapter 1 and the closing chapters 17–21 differ radically from the DH mainstream of the rest of the book. Chapter 1 presents the conquest of Canaan as unfinished, in sharp contrast to the DH presentation found in Joshua (Josh 11:23; 21:43-45). Joshua's death is reported twice (Judg 1:1 and 2:8), and Judges 2:6-10 overlaps with Joshua 24:28-31. This state of affairs suggests that Judges 1:1–2:5 was added to serve as an introduction to the book of Judges once it had been separated from DH. This added section's portrayal of an incomplete conquest that left foreigners in the land (Judg 1:21, 27, etc.) provides the context for Israel's apostasy in the final form of Judges.

Chapters 17–21 take a similarly negative perspective. According to these chapters, Israel's social and religious life broke down completely because it lacked a king to prevent self-centered, unprincipled behavior. The narratives are held firmly together by the evaluative formula, "there was no king in Israel" (Judg 17:6; 18:1; 19:1; 21:25). These concluding chapters no longer refer to the judges or to the attacks of external enemies that concern the earlier part of the book. They pay no attention to the thematic link between Samson and Samuel or the forty-year span of Philistine oppression that these two leaders divide between them (Judg 13:1; 15:20; ending with 1 Sam 7:13). These circumstances demonstrate that chapters 17–21 were added later in order to round out Judges after it had been separated from the book of Samuel.

ISSUES IN READING

Judges may be read theologically as a cautionary tale about disloyalty to God and its consequences. However, it can also be enjoyed as sophisticated literature. The reader might choose to compare the characters' contrasting personality traits as revealed by their words and actions. Recent interpreters have been inclined to explore the oppression of women and patriarchal power reflected in Judges.[3]

One anomaly inevitably strikes any reader who has moved into Judges from Joshua. As already mentioned, in contrast to the complete conquest described in Joshua (Josh 11:23; 21:43-45), Judges 1 portrays an incomplete conquest that continued after Joshua's death. Although Judah is successful, the overall failure of the other tribes (vv. 21-36) contrasts sharply with the positive picture set forth in Joshua. Thus in Judges the alien nations are left to live side-by-side with Israel in the land. We are told that Israel's failure to complete the conquest was both a punishment for their sins (2:20-21) and a test of their obedience (2:22-23; 3:1, 4). Still a third explanation is that they remained to train Israel for war (3:2).[4]

When Joshua and Judges are read together in their final, canonical forms, however, these inconsistencies are more a matter of a shift in perspective than outright contradictions. Joshua itself speaks of adversaries left in the land (Josh 15:63; 16:10; 17:12-13; 23:5, 7, 12). The upbeat perspective of Joshua portrays obedience, success, and the fulfillment of all God's promises.

Judges then moves on to the next episode of Israel's story, one marked by growing disobedience and the grim reality of struggle against neighboring foes.

The wide culture gaps that exist between the ancient audience of Judges and its modern readers make our task of interpretation much more difficult. To us, Gideon's careful rechecking of God's sign (Judg 6:36-40) sounds indecisive and timid. Yet seeking divine assurance of victory was an expected element of holy war tradition, and fleece left outside would likely be wet with dew as a matter of course. Today Jephthah's vow (11:29-40) seems criminally reckless, whereas the first readers probably understood it as a reasonable pledge stated in a foolish and thoughtless way. Moreover, the story simply assumes without question that Jephthah must keep his bloody vow, whereas modern readers have plenty of questions and objections.

Samson's exploits point to another cultural gap. They sound childish and irresponsible to us, but the original readers probably appreciated his picaresque adventures as tricky and insulting blows against the hated Philistines. In chapter 19, ancient readers would have been outraged not only by the brutal rape, murder, and dismemberment of the woman, so appalling to us, but also by the shocking lack of hospitality shown by the men of Gibeah. Another example is 21:15-23, where modern readers tend to perceive kidnapping and rape in the events described. However, the text itself presents this action as an atypical route to marriage and considers the offense as being directed against the young women's fathers and brothers, whose privilege of making decisions about marriage for their daughters and sisters has been bypassed.

It is hard to ascertain the relationship of the stories of Judges to concrete history. For one thing, there is no reason to suppose that the book presents the judges in actual chronological order. More important, folktales such as these are not really useful to the historian for establishing actual events. However they do reveal a good deal about the social history and worldview of Israel's early period.

Judges describes a loose association of small agricultural and pastoral villages or clans located in the highlands away from the main Canaanite power centers. Israel's social structure is egalitarian without wide disparities of wealth or power, but also

97

intensely patriarchal. Life is marked by xenophobia, insecurity because of enemy attacks, and recurring warfare fought from a religious perspective. Israel shares a common code of behavior that places a high value on hospitality, the protection of guests, and joining together to fight common enemies. To violate this informal code was to commit "a vile outrage in Israel" (Judg 20:6) and to invite ridicule (5:15*b*-17). Family and clan ties are more important than tribal loyalties, and the notion of a wider national unity is barely on the horizon. Only the Song of Deborah (which may represent the latest of these stories) supposes any sort of pan-tribal alliance, and that is enforced by nothing more effective than moral obligation. Israel engages in violent encounters with other peoples who live in their land or encroach upon it. They fight against city-states with an elite hierarchical ruling class and chariots (chaps. 4–5). Local elders (8:14, 16; 11:5, 11) provide day-to-day administration, but warfare presents a crisis that demands the leadership of talented and charismatic heroes (for example, 11:4-11). In broad outline, at least, this picture corresponds well with what archaeology reveals about early Iron Age Palestine.[5]

THE PLOT OF JUDGES

One way to discern the shape of a plot is to look at its beginning and ending. The question that begins the conquest in Judges 1 is "Who shall go up first" to fight, and God's answer is "Judah shall go up" (v. 1). Near the end of the book, the same question receives the same answer from God (20:18). This pairing of question and answer provides an ironic framework for the action in between. Although the questions and answers are similar, the contexts out of which they are asked and answered contrast sharply. From a worthy holy war in chapter 1, fought to carry through the conquest, in chapter 20 Israel has degenerated so far that it fights a false and tragic holy war to punish one of its own tribes. The "children of Israel" who disperse in 21:24 are in much worse circumstances than those who mustered in 1:1. Overall, the plot of Judges descends from obedience (2:7) to depravity and from at least partial military success to civil war fought with near total abandon.

Judges 1:1–3:6 functions as a section of exposition that introduces the plot of Judges. It presents the setting of time, place, and context, and describes the narrative problem. The reader quickly learns that this book is going to be about the troubled relationship between Israel and the Lord. The context for this troubled relationship is a conquest that is only partial (1:27-36; 2:21-23; 3:1-5) and Israel's habitual inclination toward disloyalty (2:1-5, 11-15, 19-21). The death of Joshua (1:1; 2:8) raises immediate questions for the reader. Who will lead Israel now that Joshua is dead? Will the people be obedient or disobedient?

The impact of Joshua's death moves Israel in two successive directions, first toward renewed conquest, but also toward apostasy. This double movement is reflected in the double mention of Joshua's death (Judg 1:1 and 2:8). Joshua 1:1 initiates a conquest reported first positively, but then increasingly as a failure. The angel at Bochim brings this movement to an end by revealing that God will no longer drive the enemy peoples out (2:1-5). Then a second report of Joshua's death (2:8) leads Israel's story into disloyal apostasy (2:10-15) and initiates the stagnant cycle that organizes the center section of the book (2:16-21).

Yet these two introductory movements are not unrelated, but are coordinated by the problem of foreign pagans in the land. Israel is caught in a vicious circle. The failed conquest means that foreigners remain to tempt Israel into disobedience (Judg 2:3), while disobedience in turn means that foreigners will continue to remain in the land (2:20-23)! This then leads to intermarriage and even further disobedience (3:1-6). The rest of Judges describes Israel's life lived out under the bleak conditions set forth in 2:3, 21-23. God's promise of a total conquest is not to be fulfilled, but God is still in charge and remains concerned with and connected to Israel.

The tales about individual judges (Judg 3:7–16:31) are little "plots within the plot" in which the dramatic tension about Israel's conflicted relationship with God repeatedly rises and falls. Overall, however, the plot direction tends to drift downward as Israel descends into ever more serious misbehavior (2:19). This decline takes place in the public arena of war and government, but also in the private arena of family life and the relationships between men and women.

The dominant plot movement operates in the public arena. There the judges play a hero's role, although they become increasingly flawed and ineffective. There is a perceptible deterioration in the quality of their leadership. Thus Othniel and Ehud are wholly positive characters, but the fortitude of Deborah and the boldness of Jael find their antithesis in the "unmanly" hesitation of Barak (Judg 4:8-9). Gideon is hardly decisive (6:13, 15) and his none-too-stalwart destruction of Baal's altar (6:27) is later offset by his dalliance with a dubious ephod (8:27). His refusal of an offer of kingship is admirable (8:22-23), but his son Abimelech grasps for royal status with a ruthlessness that results in tragedy (chap. 9). The leadership of both Gideon and Jephthah is marred by violent internal quarrels (8:1-3, 16-17; 12:1-6).

This pattern of decline is also reflected in the private arena of family and the associations between men and women. Positive developments such as Achsah's assertiveness as Othniel's suitably Israelite bride (Judg 1:11-15) are offset by the dangers of intermarriage (3:6). This tension between the sexes has its positive side in the slaying of Sisera by Jael (4:21; 5:24-27) and that of Abimelech by the woman of Thebez (9:53). Nevertheless, Jephthah's public successes are hindered by strife within his family of origin (11:1-3) and undermined by the sacrifice of his daughter (11:34-40).

Ineptitude in the public arena and the "battle of the sexes" in private life merge in the story of Samson, Israel's most colorful but least effective judge. The story of his birth and nazirite status is told in a thoroughly positive way (chap. 13). A nazirite ("dedicated one") was someone who vowed to live a special lifestyle of consecration (Numbers 6). However, Samson's exploits of "judging" (Judg 15:20) never move outside the sphere of private feud and vengeance. Samson serves as a prime illustration of the intermarriage problem referred to in 3:6. His sexual associations with enemy women (his wife, a prostitute at Gaza, and Delilah) bring about his failure. He is "into" Philistine women (both idiomatically and literally) and spends most of his time in Philistine territory. He never leads Israel into war and therefore his escapades only "begin to deliver Israel" (13:5). This breakdown in social and family values continues in the final chapters (17:1-4; 19:1-2, 15, 22-24), and violence against women (19:25-29; 21:11-12, 20-23) increasingly deforms relations between the sexes.

The trajectory by which Israel declines into disorder, disobedience, and failure, is punctuated by repeated warnings from God

(Judg 2:1-5; 6:7-10; 10:11-14), but to no avail. In contrast to the formulas of success associated with earlier judges (3:11; 3:30; 5:31; 8:28), after Gideon there are no more notices that the land "had rest." Nor are the Philistines ever "subdued" by Samson (contrast 3:30; 4:23; 8:28; 11:33).

Judges closes with a chilling description of the deterioration of Israel's religious, social, and political life in chapters 17–21. There are no more positive reports, only the violent tragedies of theft, kidnapping, lethal rape, and civil war. In the private arena, the reader encounters an idol at a private shrine, lack of hospitality, rape and murder, and irregular marriage arrangements. In the public arena, Israel has moved from having ambiguous leadership to almost no leadership at all. National leaders who advocate destructive policies have replaced the judges (Judg 20:2; 21:16). The public tribal religion of Dan is apostate and the illegitimate background of their sanctuary is emphasized at every turn: pilfered silver (17:2-3), a stolen illicit image (17:5-6; 18:16-18, 24), and an opportunistic priest (17:9; 18:19-20). Wars against Israel's foes are replaced by ludicrous imitations of holy war fought against other Israelites (chap. 20; 21:10-12).

These final negative developments come as no real surprise to the reader, for they are foreshadowed earlier in the book. Judges 1:34 introduces Dan's dilemma. The religious irregularity of Gideon's ephod in 8:27 prepares the reader for Micah's idol (17:5). The intertribal dissent that marred the successes of Gideon, Jephthah, and Samson (8:1-3; 12:1-6; 15:9-13) has reached its ultimate low point in the all-out civil war against Benjamin (chap. 20). In a more subtle way, the notion of all the people doing "what was right in their own eyes" (17:6; etc.) is foreshadowed by Samson's faithless intermarriage, for in Hebrew Samson's Philistine bride was "right" in his "eyes" (14:3, 7). Israel's self-centered errors of judgment simply continue its long-standing practice of doing what was "evil in the Lord's eyes" (2:11; 3:12; 4:1; 6:1; 10:6; 13:1; NRSV: "in the sight of the Lord").

Another way to assess the plot of Judges is to look at Israel's national tragedy from God's perspective. The six subplots about the major judges illustrate the Lord's reaction to Israel's disobedience as summarized in Judges 2:11-16. God's reaction to disloyalty is punishment; the divine response to repentance is deliverance. The Lord is emotionally involved with Israel in both anger and compassion. God can be moved to pity and a positive promise by heartfelt repentance (2:8; 10:16). However, along with God's promise come the calamitous results of divine anger. Thus from the very beginning, the story of Judges is played out within the dangerous context of neighboring enemy peoples, who were left behind as God's punishment for Israel's earlier sin (2:3, 21-23).

In Judges, God does not act in direct or unmediated ways, but works through historical and human means to bring punishment and deliverance. God punishes Israel through the hostility of enemy peoples and raises up and empowers saviors who remain completely human. God equips these leaders with the spirit (Judg 3:10; 6:34; 11:29) and with victory in holy wars, delivering the foe into their hands (e.g., 3:10, 28; 4:7). However, their success also depends in large part on their own human skills, obedience, and character. Their stories explore the question of the proper human reaction to God's call and intervention. Ehud opts for stealth. Barak hesitates. Gideon demurs, acts under the safe cover of night, seeks for signs, rejects an offer of kingship, and finally falls into idolatry. Jephthah negotiates with the enemy king, then seeks to enhance the Lord's favor with a vow that has fatal consequences. Samson exhibits a lusty indifference to his responsibility to be a nazirite and national deliverer.

From God's perspective, the balance of the plot shifts decisively in the last five chapters, in which human freedom in the worst sense dominates and human leadership has disappeared. At this point, God's own involvement in the story drops down to almost nothing. Humans make cultic arrangements for their own purposes without resort to divine guidance (chaps. 17–18). The climactic civil war is instituted not by God's spirit but by human outrage sparked by what is at least partially a lie. (Compare the Levite's testimony of Judges 20:4-6 with what is actually reported in 19:22-30.) In the end this civil war actually does turn out to be God's war too (20:28, 35), but ironically it is a holy war of divine punishment, not deliverance. Just as it does in the earlier chapters, God's act of salvation depends on human repentance, a human answer to the call of leadership, and human obedience. But now Israel has reached its nadir, and these necessary human responses are no longer present or visible.[6]

In spite of the structural techniques used to unify and integrate

Judges, the book leaves its reader with an impression of increasing confusion and chaos. That is to say, the book constantly undermines its own structures, and this fact corresponds with and amplifies the theme of increasing disobedience, dissolution, and disorder. For instance, the book never quite achieves the symmetry of a twelve-tribe nation, but keeps falling just short of this goal. One tribe, Issachar, is noticeably absent from the introductory armed conflicts of chapter 1. The horizon of the Song of Deborah (chap. 5) encompasses only ten tribes, ignoring Judah and Simeon. Although the reader seems to be encouraged to count twelve judges, actually to do so requires including either the enigmatic Shamgar (3:31) or the dubious Abimelech (chap. 9). Nor is there quite one judge per tribe, although again the book comes close to this goal (only Simeon and Reuben lack one).[7]

Overall, the plot of Judges is intensely gloomy and negative. The pessimism reflected in Judges 2:1-5, 19; 6:7-10; and 10:6-14 is heightened by the revelation that Israel will eventually go into captivity (18:30). Yet the book also points beyond itself in hope. As we have seen, God's salvation requires human commitment and effort. Because Israel has reached the lowest conceivable point in its relationship to God, it is challenged even more strongly to cry out again in repentance to the Lord. Once more the time has come to put away foreign gods (10:16).

If the repeated oscillation between apostasy and return has gotten Israel nowhere, at least this futile rhythm is broken by Samson's failure to "subdue" and bring "rest" to the land. The absence of any judge as the book ends also implies that the stagnant cycle has been interrupted. Clearly what Israel needs is a king. Abimelech's initial failure leads the reader to ask just what sort of king could succeed. Chapters 17–21 illustrate military and ethical problems that urgently call for kingship: "There was no king in Israel" (21:25), but this phrase also implies that there will eventually be one. In this way, Judges looks forward to the accomplishments of Samuel, who will subdue the Philistines and establish the monarchy.

CONTEXTS AND AUDIENCES

Judges was addressed to a preexilic audience celebrating its national identity in the face of constant threat. We meet this audience in Deborah's song as everyone rejoices in the "triumphs" of the Lord and of Israel. These include aristocrats who ride on valuable animals and sit on rich carpets, as well as ordinary folks who go on foot and gather at watering places (Judg 5:10-11). Israel needed to assert its identity as God's protected people because the nation was so often under siege and endangered by outside forces. Consequently, tales describing the heroism of local favorite sons (and one daughter) were recited over and over in story and song. Because these stories attested to Israel's possession of Palestine, they were characteristically connected to well-known geographic features of the cherished homeland: Deborah's tree (4:5), Ehud's sculptured stones (3:19, 26), Gideon's altar (6:24), and Samson's hill (15:17). They evoked familiar or remembered customs such as lamenting for Jephthah's daughter (11:39-40) and dancing at Shiloh (21:19-23). Gideon's victory over Midian was so celebrated that it became a proverbial example of the Lord's deliverance (Ps 83:9-12; Isa 9:4).

At a later point, Judges was also addressed to a sadder but wiser audience of contrite penitents. During the later monarchy period and finally in exile, God's people endured national weakness, defeat, and disgrace. Judges in its DH form provided them with an answer to the question of what had gone wrong: God has punished us because we were incessantly disloyal. We failed to keep aloof from the native population and their pagan gods, and so as a consequence we have experienced defeat (Judg 2:2-3; 6:10; 10:13-14). Judges insists that Israel's propensity for disobedience began early, almost as soon as it settled in the land. Repeatedly, Israel responded to God's gracious deliverance with renewed misbehavior and the worship of other gods: "The Israelites again did what was evil" (3:12; 4:1; etc.). Yet the repeated cyclical pattern of Judges also offered hope to this readership enduring national distress. To repent, to put away foreign gods, and to cry to the Lord might again bring deliverance (10:15-16).

It is clear that Judges is addressed to an audience made up of both men and women and exploits this fact to create irony and reader interest. For example, the story of Deborah and Barak is told at the expense of its male characters. In chapter 4, she is understood as a faithful prophet, but he is a judge who is faint of heart. As a prophet, Deborah delivers divine messages that offer Barak assurance of victory (vv. 6-7, 14), but she also chides him for his hesitancy (v. 9). Jael's "motherly" offer of a rug and milk sounds at first like courteous hospitality (vv. 18-19), but by encouraging sleep, she is setting Sisera up for the kill. Sisera's request to her reveals his unmanly fear (v. 20). She is to answer "no" to a question that in Hebrew literally reads, "Is there a man here?" Hammering tent pegs would have been a routine task for a nomadic woman (v. 21), but here it takes a lethal twist. This exploration of men's and women's roles continues at the end of Judges 5. The penetrating tent peg and Sisera's fall "between her feet" (the literal Hebrew of 5:27; NRSV "at her feet") have sexual implications. This appears to be a reversal of the battlefield rape alluded to in verse 30, which was (and is) often women's lot in war. With delicious sarcasm, the poet describes Sisera's mother waiting in vain. Her son is not out ravishing captive girls (v. 30), but has been ravished himself. It is quite typical that later religious tradition tended to forget Deborah and remember Barak (1 Sam 12:11; Heb 11:32)!

Abimelech also dies by a woman's hand (Judg 9:53-54). An "upper millstone" was an item commonly used by women. Although Abimelech seeks to avoid the notoriety of being killed by a woman (4:9), he actually becomes a proverbial example of such a death (2 Sam 11:21).

A concern for gender relationships again appears in the story of Jephthah's unnamed daughter (Judg 11:29-40). His vow is rash, careless, and egocentric, although his words do not necessarily specify that his sacrifice would be a human being (vv. 30-31; NRSV "whoever" could also be "whatever"). Israelites often shared their houses with farm animals. Nevertheless, his daughter does a completely expected and predictable thing by coming out to him, for Israelite women customarily celebrated victories (Exod 15:20-21; 1 Sam 18:6-7). He is distraught, but also sounds as though he is blaming her (Judg 11:35). In sharp contrast, she is courageous and devout, and seizes control of how she will spend the last months of her life (vv. 36-37).

The "battle of the sexes" reaches near comic levels in the misadventures of Samson. Even when his birth is announced to his parents, the reader notices that his mother is a good deal more perceptive about what is going on than his father (Judg 13:6-7 over against v. 8). Samson's sexual longings entice him into marriage with the enemy (14:1-3; cf. 3:6). His Philistine wife, seeking to save herself and her family (v. 15), has little trouble in discovering the secret of his riddle (vv. 16-17). Her persistent and effective argument ("You do not really love me") works equally well for Delilah (16:15-17), whose astute use of psychology "cuts short" the career of Israel's last judge.

Things move from near comedy to complete tragedy in the last chapters. The rape of the Levite's concubine in chapter 19 censures the men of Gibeah. The powerful description of their violation of her and the poignant final scene at the door fuel the reader's outrage against them (Judg 19:25-26). However, the story also denounces her cowardly Levite husband, who acts dishonorably to save himself (v. 25) and then lies about it (20:5). The affecting image of her "hands on the threshold" is in sharp contrast to his brusque unconcern (19:27-28). He treats her body as a disposable object, merely a signal to rally the nation (vv. 29-30; cf. 1 Sam 11:7). The resulting civil war nearly exterminates Benjamin and ushers in two scandalous schemes to obtain wives for them outside socially acceptable channels (21:8-14, 19-23). These ill-fated young women are torn away from their protecting male family members, first by a vicious massacre and then by kidnapping. It is both ethically and theologically significant that the ultimate collapse of Israel's relationship with God carries with it a similar breakdown of the just and proper relationship between the sexes.[8]

THEMES

Leadership

Judges offers an exploration of various leadership styles under the ultimate direction of God. Deborah is a judge in the juridical sense who decides cases for the people, but she is also a prophet who speaks God's word to motivate and chastise her associate Barak (Judg 4:4-7, 9, 14). The other judges are local saviors who move with local tribal resources against local foes. The enemies of the judges tend to be geographically nearby: Moab to Ehud of Benjamin, Hazor to the Galilee tribes of Zebulun and Naphtali led by Barak, the Ammonites to Jephthah of Gilead, the Philistines to

106

Samson the Danite. The minor judges, on the other hand, conduct their office with reference to Israel as a whole. The verb "judge" covers the activities of all these leaders: to govern and deliver, to rescue, and vindicate. Some are less successful than others, based on their obedience and character.

In contrast, dynastic kingship based on human choice leads only to strife and violence. When Gideon is offered hereditary rule, his answer ("The LORD will rule over you") expresses Israel's traditional notion that choosing human kings impinges on the Lord's kingship (Judg 8:23; 1 Sam 8:7). Israel's experience with Abimelech demonstrates the destructive side of kingship, and Jotham's fable (Judg 9:7-21) displays a cynicism about kingship similar to that found in 1 Samuel 8.[9] All the useful plants refuse kingship as a waste of their valuable aptitudes. The worthless bramble accepts, but its shade is prickly and meager and its potential for fire threatens danger. In the end, however, Judges asserts that only a king can bring public order to the chaos that inevitably results from unrestrained self-interest. Rape, civil war, genocide—all occurred because Israel had no king.

The Spirit of the Lord

God empowers the judges through spirit, the animating force of God's personality that falls on those chosen for some special responsibility. The Lord bestows this numinous energy on Othniel (Judg 3:10) and Gideon (6:34), but not on Ehud or Deborah. The spirit comes into view only belatedly for Jephthah (11:29), perhaps as a reflection of God's greater displeasure with Israel at this point (10:11-14) or because Jephthah owed his position to human initiative (11:10-11). The spirit of the Lord appears four times in the Samson story, providing a coordinating theme for the different episodes. Although the spirit gives the other judges leadership abilities, on Samson it confers superhuman strength. The Lord's spirit is only latent in 13:25, promising great feats to come. In 14:5-6, 19; 15:14-15 it is the motive power behind his feats of strength. A different notion of his God-given vigor appears in chapter 16. When Samson loses his hair, he loses his dedicated status as a nazirite (13:5) and his strength along with it. His powers return as his hair grows back and his nazirite status is restored (16:22).

107

Holy War

The holy war tradition describes the belief that the Lord guided Israelite armies in battle and fought for them in the capacity of divine warrior. The divine warrior was a common concept in the ancient world. It depicted a given nation's god leading heavenly armies into battle and fighting with supernatural weapons. The Lord's guidance in tactics and a divine assurance of victory were critical elements in Israel's holy war tradition (Judg 4:6-7). According to 5:20-21, the stars fought for Israel and the Kishon River overwhelmed the enemy. Panic is the most characteristic weapon of the divine warrior (4:15), and Gideon's victory over Midian is the best-known example of this (7:21-22). In holy war, the Lord alone wins the victory. The requirement that Gideon should send home most of his army underscores this point (7:2-3, 7-8). Holy war also implied the complete slaughter of the enemy as spoil to be devoted to the Lord for destruction (1:17).[10]

The Israelites' conviction that the Lord fought as divine warrior in their behalf was significant and comforting, because their enemies often outclassed them. Chariots with iron fittings gave the Canaanites battlefield superiority outside the broken terrain of Palestine's hill country (Judg 1:19), and camels gave Midianite raiders superior mobility over long distances (7:12).

Judges concludes tragically with a reversed holy war against the tribe of Benjamin (chap. 20). As in the case of an ordinary holy war, the participants take a war vow (20:8; 21:1), ask the Lord's guidance (vv. 18, 21), and receive divine assurance of victory (v. 28). The tactics of ambush and simulated retreat (v. 33) parallel those of Joshua 8:3-23. The outcome, however, is calamitous. One of Israel's tribes is nearly annihilated (20:46-47; 21:3). Judges contrasts this upside-down holy war with the proper sort using an ironic parallel with the holy war question-and-answer schema that opens the book (1:1; 20:18). It serves as further evidence that Israel's relationship with the Lord has nearly collapsed.

CHAPTER 7

THE BOOKS OF
1 AND 2
SAMUEL

SHAPES AND STRUCTURES

Samuel is not a well-organized book. Overall it follows the overlapping stories of its three most important characters: Samuel alone (1 Samuel 1–8), Samuel and Saul (1 Samuel 9–15), Saul and David (1 Samuel 16–2 Samuel 1), and David alone (2 Samuel 2–24). More than half of 1 and 2 Samuel is dedicated to the topic of David's kingdom. This description of David can be further subdivided into David's story under the power of blessing (2 Samuel 2–8) followed by his story under the power of curse (2 Samuel 9–24). Second Samuel 5:12 summarizes the blessing phase of David's story. The curse subdivision centers on the consequences of Nathan's threat spoken in 12:10-12. Dark tragedy almost overwhelms David's throne and family, but the Lord remains engaged with him until the end.

However, this outline does not correspond very well to the book's various summary statements, which cut across these divisions. What sound like summary paragraphs occur at:

- 1 Samuel 7:15-17 (Samuel as judge)
- 1 Samuel 14:47-52 (Saul's reign)
- 2 Samuel 8:15-18 (David's reign)
- 2 Samuel 20:23-26 (David's officials).

Other transitional points seem to be indicated by

- 1 Samuel 12:1-25 (Samuel's farewell)
- 1 Samuel 13:1 (introduction to Saul's reign)
- 2 Samuel 1:1 ("after the death of Saul")
- 2 Samuel 5:4-5 (introduction to David's reign).

This disarray is the result of a long and complex process of editing and supplementing. Different themes and purposes became dominant in successive stages of the growth of the book. In spite of this, Samuel can still be read as a coherent whole without too much trouble.

The Ark Story

The contours of three independent sources used to construct the book of Samuel are still visible to the attentive reader. The first of these is the Ark Story (1 Sam 4:1–7:1 and 2 Sam 6:1-19). This describes the itinerary of the ark of the covenant from its battlefield capture by the Philistines to its installation by David in Jerusalem. The two halves of this narrative whole are linked by a common content, portraying the journey of the ark and its effects on those around it. The second part picks up the ark's story where the first part left it, at "the house of Abinadab" (1 Sam 7:1 and 2 Sam 6:3).

The ark is wrested from its traditional home in Shiloh and transported on a circuit of three Philistine cities. Then the Philistines send it back to Judah where it remains in "cold storage" for twenty years until David transfers it to the recently captured city of Jerusalem. At each stage of its journey, the ark reacts powerfully in response to its environment.

Taken into battle by the distraught Israelites, it permits itself to be captured (1 Sam 4:4, 11). However, in each Philistine city to which it is moved, it performs hostile deeds. In Ashdod it insults the local god Dagon (5:3-4) and plagues the population with tumors (v. 6). Quickly packed off to Gath, "the hand of the Lord" causes panic and more tumors (v. 9). When the people of Gath send it on to Ekron, again there is panic and deadly plague (v. 11). Repeated mention of the Lord's "hand" makes it clear that the effects of the presence of the ark are a direct result of the Lord's purposes. Ironically, the Philistines had initially feared the Lord's hand when the ark first appeared in Israel's camp (4:8; NRSV: "power"). However, by capturing the ark they have succeeded only in bringing the deadly weight of that "hand" upon themselves (5:6, 7, 9, 11). It is no accident that when the idol of Dagon falls before the ark, it loses its hands as well as its head (5:4).

The Philistines wisely decide to get rid of this hazardous object and avoid this pestilent divine "hand" (1 Sam 6:3, 5, 9). They devise a plan to placate the ark with offerings and to let it decide for itself where it would like to go (6:3-9). The ark heads straight back to Beth-shemesh in the land of Israel, but even there it causes a catastrophe (6:19). So it is transported one stage closer toward home, then remains quietly in Kiriath-jearim for twenty years (7:1). When David plans to take the ark to Jerusalem, a foolish error causes a catastrophe that makes David hesitate and prompts him to leave the ark at a house along the way (2 Sam 6:6-10). However, blessings showered on that household soon persuade David to continue with his plan (vv. 11-12), and the ark proceeds to its new home in Jerusalem.

Some traditionalists in Israel apparently believed that the ark properly belonged in its ancient home in Shiloh and certainly not in the previously foreign and pagan city of Jerusalem. The Ark Story clearly seeks to counter such an opinion by asserting that David's scheme to move it to his new capital was unquestionably God's will.[1]

The Rise of David

This second independent source, found in 1 Samuel 16:14–2 Samuel 5:12, recounts that the Lord began the process of transferring kingship from Saul to David even during Saul's lifetime. Its editorial theme can be expressed in the phrase, Saul must decrease and David must increase. Saul is abandoned by the spirit of the Lord and is instead tormented by a spirit of depression and morbid suspicion (1 Sam 16:14). Parallel stories explain how young David first arrives at Saul's court, either as a therapeutic musician (16:15-23) or as a war hero (chap. 17; note that v. 55

indicates that Saul does not know who David is). David's growing popularity inflames Saul's jealousy (18:6-11). The reader is told repeatedly that the Lord has left Saul, and now is with David instead (18:12, 14, 28).

David is loved by Saul's daughter and son Jonathan (1 Sam 18:1-4, 28; 20:17), but Saul becomes his fearful enemy (18:29). Acts of increasing desperation testify to Saul's deterioration. He repeatedly attempts to cause David's death (18:20-29; 19:9-17). He takes bloody vengeance on an entire priestly family (22:11-19). Because God no longer communicates with him, Saul desperately attempts to learn the future from Samuel's ghost (28:3-25).

At the same time, the career of David moves in the opposite direction, ever upward. He escapes death with the help of Saul's own children (1 Sam 19:11-17; 20:1-42). Beginning as a fugitive with a band of desperate outlaws (22:1-2), he wins military successes (23:1-5; 27:8-11; 30:1-31), eludes Saul at every turn (23:6-28), and enjoys the protection of Saul's enemies (21:10-15; 27:1-7). He gains riches and wives (chap. 25). Twice (chaps. 24 and 26) David virtuously spares the life of Saul, who as anointed king was considered inviolable (24:6, 10; 26:9, 11, 23). Even Saul comes to recognize that the future lies with David (26:25).

After Saul's death by suicide (1 Samuel 31), David innocently benefits from the violence and treachery of others (2 Sam 3:6-30; 4:5-12). First Judah (2:1-7) and then Israel (5:1-5) chooses him as king. In the end, after capturing Jerusalem, David perceives that the Lord has established him as king (2 Sam 5:12). God has exalted the lowly shepherd boy (1 Sam 16:19) to the exalted position of shepherd king (2 Sam 5:2). The purpose of this ancient piece of historiography was to establish the divine legitimacy of David's kingship over against the family of Saul and defend his dynasty against charges that he had illegitimately usurped Saul's throne. "David became greater and greater, for the LORD, the God of hosts, was with him" (5:10).

The Throne Succession Story

Second Samuel 9–20 and 1 Kings 1–2, the third independent source, recount the palace intrigues and family struggles that led to Solomon's attainment of his father David's throne. Scholars variously label this older source the Throne Succession Story, the

Court History of David, or the Succession Narrative. The theme of this literary work is focused by a phrase spoken to David near its conclusion: "Who shall sit on the throne of my lord the king after him" (1 Kgs 1:20).

The reader quickly learns that royal sovereignty will not pass down through the house of Saul. Saul's grandson Mephibosheth is presumably disqualified from kingship by his physical infirmity and is kept under tight surveillance (2 Sam 9:13). In an earlier scene (which may also be part of the Throne Succession Story), the reader has discovered that David's wife Michal, who as Saul's daughter could have given birth to a grandson of Saul to succeed as king, "had no child to the day of her death" (2 Sam 6:23). Solomon comes on the scene as the offspring of David's dubious marriage to Bathsheba (12:24-25). The reader is put on notice that there will be violence and misfortune in David's household as a result of his adultery with her and his murder of her first husband (12:10-12). However, Solomon is a different matter. For some unexplained reason "the LORD loved him" from birth (12:24).

Each of David's older sons by other women is eliminated one by one. Amnon rapes his half-sister Tamar and is exiled and eventually killed by her full brother Absalom (2 Samuel 13). Absalom engages in a nearly successful revolt against his father David that in the end leads to his death (chaps. 14–18). Adonijah also desires his father's kingship (1 Kgs 1:5), but is outmaneuvered by Solomon's supporters, who portray a festival he hosts as a treacherous bid for the throne (vv. 11, 18-19, 25). After a short co-regency with his father, Solomon's succession is solidly established by a purge of his political enemies (1 Kgs 2:13-46).

This historiographic report appears to have been produced as propaganda to support the succession of Solomon against whatever forces or opinions may have opposed it. At the same time, it was clearly also intended to entertain its readership. In this way it is reminiscent of a modern historical novel. It displays great literary artistry and psychological insight, the latter exhibited in episodes such as 2 Samuel 13:1-19; 17:1-14; 18:19-33. As is typical of biblical historiography, God's will is understood to be the chief causative factor behind events. However, in the Throne Succession Story, the Lord operates in a hidden way behind the scenes, usually revealed to the reader only by the observations of the one who tells the story. The Lord is displeased by David's sin (11:27) and raises evil against David from his own house (12:11). The Lord loves Solomon from the moment of his birth (12:24). The Lord turns Absalom against the good advice of his counselor Ahithophel to follow the absurd advice given by David's undercover agent Hushai (17:14), and consequently Absalom is ruined.

The Throne Succession Story displays an astonishingly critical attitude toward David. The nemesis of divine judgment works itself out in the sex and violence endemic in his family (cf. 2 Sam 12:11 with 16:22). There is no human glory in how Solomon comes to the throne over the dead bodies of his rivals. However, the work's contention is not that David and Solomon were noble or virtuous characters, but only that the Lord graciously chose them to be Israel's kings.[2]

ISSUES IN READING

Samuel can be a perplexing book because the complex history of its composition did not completely silence the opinions of earlier sources. The authors and editors have processed previously existing traditions into a rough-hewn final product, but the older traditions continue to be visible in the mix. Antithetical voices continue to speak. Old debates over the Jerusalem Temple and the value of the monarchy may seem to have been settled in the final form of Samuel, but earlier voices advocating other positions have not been forgotten or completely silenced. One of Samuel's most puzzling features is that it presents views opposing the monarchy side-by-side with views supporting it. Passages favorable to kingship (1 Sam 9:1–10:16; 11:1-15) are interleaved in a confusing mix with ones unfavorable to it (8:1-22; 10:17-27; 12:1-25). (The question of the monarchy is taken up in the discussion under "Themes.")

The relationship of Samuel to factual history remains a disputed issue. Given their highly theological character, it is difficult to use the materials preserved in Samuel to write history in a direct fashion. For example, the portrayal of Saul presents several enigmas. Is the short length of his reign given in 1 Samuel 13:1 (two years) believable, or has this passage suffered textual corruption? Would it be better to think of Saul as a chieftain or "strong man" rather than a full-fledged king in the later sense?

How large was his kingdom, considering his successor's modest territory (2 Sam 2:9)? Did it include Judah? Nor is the candid historian in much better shape when it comes to David, since neither the Rise of David nor the Throne Succession Story can be dated with any degree of confidence. Some have insisted that these sources originated close to the times on which they report. Others have pointed out that promoting the significance of David would have been a fitting literary goal at any time during the monarchy of Judah.

THE PLOT OF SAMUEL

The poems near the beginning and end of Samuel perform an important role in structuring the plot. The first (1 Sam 2:1-10) is Hannah's song sung in response to God's gift of her son Samuel. Near the book's end David sings a psalm of thanksgiving (2 Sam 22:2-51), which is followed by David's last words in poetic form (23:1-7). Verbal and thematic parallels in these poems point to important issues pursued in the narratives that come in between them. Hannah begins Samuel by testifying to what the Lord can do and will do. David concludes the book by giving thanks for the victories and promises the Lord has granted him. These two singers invite the reader to explore the subject of God as the decisive actor in Israel's history, who performs acts of transformation. God's transforming acts are especially visible in the deliverance of Israel under Samuel and Saul and in David's meteoric rise to power and subsequent collapse into misfortune. Hannah first sings and David later echoes:

• "There is no Rock like our God" (1 Sam 2:2); "the Rock of Israel has said" (2 Sam 23:3).
• God "kills and brings to life" (1 Sam 2:6); "he drew me out of mighty waters" (2 Sam 22:17).
• God "brings low, he also exalts" (1 Sam 2:7); "you deliver a humble people, but your eyes are upon the haughty to bring them down" (2 Sam 22:28).
• God "will thunder in heaven" (1 Sam 2:10); "the LORD thundered from heaven" (2 Sam 22:14).
• God "will give strength to his king" (1 Sam 2:10); "he is a tower of salvation for his king" (2 Sam 22:51).

Samuel presents the reader with a complex and interwoven story line best understood as a succession of three overlapping trajectories centered on its three main characters, Samuel, Saul, and David. The trajectory of each character is launched with a story of divine call and authorization. The "launch points" for Saul (1 Samuel 9) and David (1 Samuel 16) both take place during the lifetime of Samuel, so there are periods of overlap or changeover during which two characters share the stage at the same time.

Samuel's life is presented generally positively: divinely instituted birth, call to office, leadership successes. Although the people's demand for a king and the crimes of his sons cast a pessimistic shadow, his trajectory of success rises to a plateau and remains there until death (1 Sam 7:15-17; 25:1). In contrast, disobedience and faithlessness quickly undermine Saul's meteoric rise, so that the greater part of his story represents a drawn-out decline to tragic defeat on Mount Gilboa. The story of David is more ambiguous than that of reliable Samuel or ill-fated Saul. He rises from shepherd boy to heroic and successful king. At that point he moves into a more equivocal situation, caught in a snarl of wrongdoing, divine forgiveness, and punishment in the form of family dissension. Samuel thus presents its readers with three scenarios of human life before God: the faithful and obedient saint, the tragic and despairing transgressor, and the individual who struggles with the ambiguities of life lived out where sin and faith overlap.

These three biographical trajectories have been woven together to form a single story of national progress. At the start of the book, God calls Samuel into a chaotic situation identical to that of the end of the book of Judges. Religion was corrupt (1 Sam 2:12-17, 22-25), "the word of the LORD was rare" (3:1), the Philistine foe dominated the scene. As the story unfolds, there are many ups and downs and many places where the reader is left in perplexity, but by the end of the book the Lord has brought Israel into a better situation. Israel is a settled kingdom with an anointed king both chosen and forgiven by the Lord. All enemies are held at bay (2 Sam 7:1). The ark has been relocated to Jerusalem where it belongs (6:17; 15:24-29), and David has built a proper altar there (24:25).

Samuel

Although Samuel does not die until 1 Samuel 25:1, his career is almost entirely reported in 1 Samuel 1–8 where he is the central character, chapters 9–15 where he shares the limelight with Saul, and chapter 16, which he shares with David. Biblical literature often signals a new beginning in God's interaction with Israel by telling about birth to a barren woman. Therefore, it is not surprising that this book starts with an intervention by the Lord that gives new life to Hannah, who prays in faith and responds in faith. Her song (2:1-10) praises the Lord's power to turn human life and human history topsy-turvy. In this way, her own personal experience becomes a paradigm for the upcoming story of Israel, and her son Samuel will be the one to initiate God's new future.

The priestly house of Eli is careless and corrupt (1 Sam 2:12-17), but a prophet announces its decline and eventual replacement by a new priestly house (vv. 27-36). The word of the Lord was rare (3:1), but Samuel is called as a trustworthy prophet (3:20–4:1) to announce words of admonition and judgment. The "unholy war" of the ark's capture is soon reversed by the ark's manifestation of power in Philistia, revealing that it is the Lord who is the decisive force in the history of nations (chaps. 4–6). The warlike Philistines dominate Israel at the moment, but the Lord as divine warrior will give Israel victory through Samuel (chap. 7).

In a literary sense, the wicked sons of Eli function as a foil for Hannah's son. The text alternates notices about Eli's sons (1 Sam 2:12-17, 22-25, 27-29) with remarks about Samuel (2:18-21, 26) to make this contrast clear. The figure of Samuel invites the reader to look backward. As a faithful nazirite (1:11), he is the positive counterpart to Samson and completes the judging task begun by him (7:13-14). Samuel leads the nation into the repentance necessary for deliverance according to the pattern of Judges (1 Sam 7:3-6). The reader is also directed forward in time. Samuel as a triumphant leader in holy war (vv. 10-11) serves as a forerunner of both Saul's overall failure and David's ambiguous successes.[3] Samuel's victory demonstrates that God could deliver Israel without the king the people faithlessly will demand in chapter 8. Their relationship with the Lord could have taken another and better path than that of kingship. On the other hand, the behavior of Samuel's sons (8:1-3) does not inspire the reader's confidence about a future without a king.

Both the good and bad sides of kingship in general and Saul's kingship in particular are presented in alternating vignettes (1 Sam 8:1-22; 10:17-27; 12:1-25 and 9:1–10:16; 11:1-15). Samuel makes it clear that Israel's request for a king was a grave and foolish sin. To embrace a king is plainly to "reject" the Lord (8:7; 10:19). However, in the end the Lord accepts kingship as an inevitable development and makes it part of Israel's future for either good or ill (12:13-15, 25). The Lord's gracious choice of Israel outweighs their defiance in demanding a king. Consequently, Samuel as prophet acts by God's authority to designate and anoint Saul (9:1–10:27). Nevertheless, Samuel's final address in chapter 12 casts a dark shadow over Saul. Samuel's profession of personal innocence presents a direct contrast to what one may expect of kings (cf. 12:3-5 with 8:11-18), and his final words suggest a dire future (12:25, "swept away").

Saul

The career of Saul encompasses 1 Samuel 9–15 (with Samuel) and 1 Samuel 16–2 Samuel 1 (with David). His advent and rise is reported in several stories that can be taken together to describe a somewhat unified plot movement. The people's request for a king (1 Samuel 8) leads to a confidential ceremony of anointing (9:1–10:8) that is privately confirmed by a sign for Saul (10:9-13), but publicly remains a secret (10:14-16). Then Samuel openly designates Saul as king (10:17-24), but not everyone accepts this move (10:27). Finally, Saul's military success leads to universal acclamation (11:1-15). Although the institution of kingship was originally the people's choice, Saul himself is unmistakably the Lord's choice (contrast 8:18 with 9:16; 10:1, 24). The Lord has turned hearts to make this happen (10:9, 26), and Saul is every inch a king (10:23)!

Although in 1 Samuel 8:11-18, Samuel had warned about the ways kings may be expected to act, Samuel's action in writing down the royal duties (10:25) suggests a glimmer of hope that Saul might turn out to be different. Like the judges of previous generations, Saul is permeated by God's spirit and leads a successful holy war (11:6).[4] Samuel's farewell speech (chapter 12) marks the end of the era of the judges and signals that Israel's move into the era of monarchy is complete. Thus, 13:1 provides Saul with the royal introductory formula that will introduce the reigns of the kings to follow.

However, any hopes the reader may have about Saul immediately collapse as disobedience and folly undercut his early victories. Samuel's demand in 1 Samuel 10:8 that Saul wait for him at Gilgal has already created an opportunity for disobedience. In chapter 13, Saul disobeys Samuel's command and follows this with a foolish and dangerous oath in chapter 14. Then in chapter 15, he violates the law that called for the sweeping destruction of all people and booty captured in holy war. None of this is excusable (in spite of the defenses put forth in 13:11-12; 15:15, 20-21), for Samuel's commands in 10:8 and 15:3 were unambiguously clear. Saul's own son Jonathan serves as a positive foil to his father's shortcomings. He is successful (13:3; 14:15, 23), faithful (14:6), and sensible (14:29-30). The inescapable consequence of all this is that the Lord "rejects" Saul (15:23; 16:1; cf. 8:7; 10:15) and chooses another king (13:13-14 and 15:28).

Saul's catastrophic fall from grace is a fateful tragedy with Shakespearean overtones. On one level, Saul is unquestionably held responsible for what happens to him (1 Sam 15:23, 26). For example, his rash oath in 14:24 leads directly to the people's sin of eating captured animals without properly draining the blood (vv. 31-33). Yet, his destiny as one rejected by God is also never completely explained. Saul is consumed by events only partially under his control or for which he could reasonably be held responsible. Much about God's relationship with him remains unfathomable, and God's motives remain largely hidden from the reader just as they are from Saul. The abrupt departure of the Lord's spirit from his life (16:14) is never justified or explained. It is simply that his doom is utterly sealed, as David himself later informs the reader (26:10).

In the end it is God's complete silence that makes it impossible for Saul to continue as a holy war leader and drives him to consult a medium (1 Samuel 28). Yet even then, all he hears is an implacable announcement of defeat and death. "The LORD has turned from you and become your enemy" and "torn the kingdom out of your hand, and given it to your neighbor" (28:16-17). The story of Saul hits bottom in defeat, suicide, and disgrace (31:4-10). Yet even if God has abandoned him, his rival David and those whom he had delivered choose to honor his memory in death (vv. 11-13; 2 Sam 1:17-27).

David

Samuel's last important act is to anoint David as king (1 Sam 16:1-13). In contrast to what was related about Saul's accession to kingship, this narrative is a completely unambiguous declaration of direct divine choice (16:1, 12), combined with an element of inexplicable divine sovereignty (16:6-7). The career of David is described first as an ascending counter theme to Saul's decline (1 Samuel 16–2 Samuel 1), then as a king and dynasty under God's blessing (2 Samuel 2–8), and finally as a king reigning under a curse (2 Samuel 9–24).

David's rise is recounted as the direct counterpart of Saul's decline. The advent of the Lord's spirit on David is sharply contrasted with the removal of the same spirit from Saul (1 Sam 16:13-14). The supplanting "evil spirit" that infects Saul (in modern terms a troubled psychological state) is first of all the basis of David's arrival at court (vv. 15-18, 23), then later a catalyst for Saul's animosity to him (18:10-11; 19:9-10). The basis for David's rise is the Lord's favor and protection, as the reader eventually learns from his wife-to-be Abigail (1 Sam 25:28-31). (For observations on the plot of this portion of David's story, see the foregoing discussion "The Rise of David.")

After Saul's death, the earlier pattern of rise for David and fall for Saul continues for their respective "houses" (2 Sam 3:1). David prospers because of the Lord's direction (2:1) and purpose (3:9-10, 18; 5:10, 12). However, his success also results from thoroughly human factors such as Abner's intrigue (3:12, 17-19), the dynastic significance of Saul's daughter Michal (3:13-16), the assassination of Saul's successor (4:1-8), and David's attentiveness to good public relations (3:31-37; 4:9-12). The Lord grants David the holy war victories over the Philistines that had earlier been denied to Saul (5:19-25). David's ascendancy over Saul is capped by his triumph over Saul's dynasty, which will play no further role in the royal succession (6:20-23).

The career of David reaches its high point with the transfer of the ark to Jerusalem and Nathan's oracle promising him an everlasting dynasty (2 Samuel 6–7). Religious and political centralization are fully in place: Two kingdoms have become one with one new capital city. Wars of national unification and liberation (chaps. 2–5) are followed by victories on the international scene (chaps. 8, 10). King and nation enjoy security and peace (7:1), and

David reigns victoriously and properly (8:14-15). Things will soon deteriorate, but the Lord's promise delivered by the prophet Nathan in chapter 7 explores the future implications of this transitory interval of blessing.

God's promise in 2 Samuel 7:1-17 expands the plot horizon into a limitless future. It shifts the reader's focus from the bygone tent sanctioned by tradition (vv. 6-7) to a new projected temple (v. 13) and from David as an individual to the unfolding of his dynasty (vv. 11, 16). The promises of verses 9-11 affirm that God intends to stay connected with David and his house no matter what happens.

This divine commitment is astonishing, given the negative opinions about kingship expressed earlier in the book. The Lord's promise appears to be unconditional and eternal, even in the face of all too predictable royal disobedience. It points beyond the confines of the book of Samuel itself into an unbounded future. Thus in 2 Samuel 7:23-24, David notifies readers that the eternal promise made to him also has vital significance for them, for the Lord has established a covenant of mutual relationship with Israel forever.

However, by introducing the topics of succession and disobedience (2 Sam 7:14-15), Nathan's oracle also serves as a preliminary warning to the reader that curse is about to replace blessing in David's story. Moreover, the promise of succession by a single designated offspring (vv. 14-16) raises a question. Who, of all the sons cataloged in 3:2-5 and 5:13-16, will succeed David?

In 2 Samuel 11–12, the career of David moves under the shadow of a curse. This curse drives the plot of the rest of the book. A sharp tension vibrates between Nathan's moral parable spotlighting David's murder and adultery (12:1-7) and the prophet's earlier forecast of open-ended divine promise (chap. 7). In cutting contrast to David's flippant dismissal of the haphazard character of the sword (11:25), the sword that was David's instrument of murder (12:9) now becomes the instrument of divine retribution. The sword will never depart from David's house; trouble will arise from within the royal household itself (vv. 10-11). Consequently, the first baby born from his illicit union with Bathsheba dies (vv. 15-23). Then rape, fratricide, and rebellion boil up out of his damaged family system. Factions supporting the interests of Saul's tribe and family present a continuing problem (16:5-13; 20:1-22). Ultimately of course, it is the Lord who has brought this curse about (12:1, 7-12, 15), but despite this, David remains a man of hopeful, commendable faith (12:16-23; 15:25-26, 31; 16:12).

These family quarrels again raise the issue of succession. This question is introduced indirectly in the story told by the wise woman of Tekoa (2 Sam 14:7) and then explicitly through Absalom's claim to David's kingship (15:10; 16:21-22). Although the book of Samuel never definitely identifies which son will inherit David's throne, the reader gets a strong hint that it will be Solomon (12:24). (For additional observations on the plot of this portion of David's story, see the foregoing discussion "Throne Succession Story.")

David's destiny under the curse reaches its lowest point in the death of his son Absalom and his poignant reaction to it (2 Sam 18:33). From this point on the plot of Samuel takes a turn for the better, and David begins to put the pieces of his shattered kingdom back together (chaps. 19–20). The theme of ambiguity about the proper place of kingship in Israel, first emphasized in the reports of Saul's accession and reign, continues to remain strong at the end of the book. An artfully constructed conclusion (21–24) provides a final appraisal of the equivocal value of kingship and highlights David's ambiguous situation before God.

These last four chapters celebrate royal authority, but also make it wholly subservient to God's paramount goals and power. The two narrative portions (2 Sam 21:1-14 and 24:1-25) portray similar cases of national adversity. Both conclude with the Lord's willingness to respond to "supplications for the land" (21:14; 24:25) because of David's actions. In the first story, David must tie up some loose ends inherited from Saul by permitting suitable reprisals and implementing honorable burial. In the second, David (eventually) submerges his royal pride and ambition to God's enigmatic purposes, while at the same time preparing the groundwork for the temple foreseen by Nathan (7:13).

The pair of parallel sections that center on military exploits (2 Sam 21:15-22 and 23:8-39) reaffirm the reign of David as an age of heroic triumph. However, they also suggest that there are ambiguities and limits to the king's role in bestowing victory (21:17; 23:15-17). Similarly, 2 Samuel 21:19 raises doubts in the reader's mind about who really killed Goliath, David or Elhanan (cf. 1 Samuel 17).

David's two concluding poems (22:1-51[5] and 23:1-7) summarize and comment on everything that the book of Samuel has reported.

The Lord has turned history upside down (22:26-28). The Lord has chosen and exalted David (23:1) and in the role of divine warrior (22:8-16) has delivered him from his foes (22:17-20, 30-49). David has been rewarded just as a righteous king should be (22:21-25; 23:3-4), and the Lord will support David's dynasty forever (22:51; 23:5). (For further observations on the plot of this concluding section, see chapter 3, under "Reading As Story.")

In comparison with its more superficial treatments of the exemplary figure of Samuel or the tragic personality of Saul, the book of Samuel takes the reader deep into the character of David. The narrative follows him upward from youthful hero to fortunate king, but then downward to a beleaguered man with a curse over his head, for whom almost nothing goes right. The reader experiences David's lust, his anguish over the mortal illness of a son, his distress over flight from Jerusalem, his tears over Absalom's death. His story explores the classic theme of the interplay of human free will with predestined fate. David freely chooses adultery and murder by proxy, but then finds himself trapped in a web of inescapable consequences (the "curse"). Ultimately, he overcomes his adversaries and comes to a place of maturity as the Lord's anointed. In the end, he can sing about the Lord's overarching purpose in choosing and supporting him (2 Sam 22:1–23:7). He can concede his own failings (24:10, 14, 17) and repent with appropriate sacrifices, confident in the Lord's merciful character.

The God of the story of David is equally fascinating as a literary character. This God is engaged deeply in human affairs, sometimes so deeply as to be nearly hidden. God's purposes remain largely unrevealed (e.g., 2 Sam 12:24; 24:1), but God remains enduringly committed to Israel (7:24) and to the family of David (22:51).

CONTEXTS AND AUDIENCES

The wide spectrum of viewpoints presented in Samuel suggests that it spoke to a variety of audiences during the long process of its composition. The inconsistent opinions it expresses, especially about kingship, certainly represent changes of attitude over time, but probably also delineate the conflicting views of factions within Israel that existed at the same time. Contrasting opinions about kingship probably reflect tensions between upper-class elitists and the common folk whose heavy taxes supported the royal establishment. The interpreter can also trace the opinions of Judah in collision with those of the northern tribes, especially in the conflicting evaluations of Benjamin's tribal hero Saul. There is also evidence of antagonism between supporters of Jerusalem temple worship and northern traditionalists who supported Shiloh.

Another factor contributing to the complexity of the book is its wholesale inclusion of earlier works, each of which had once spoken to a different audience. Nevertheless, to each successive generation of readers, Samuel strongly asserted the Lord's faithful engagement in Israel's political life and called readers to renew their allegiance to the Lord.

At one point Samuel existed as a part of the Deuteronomistic History and was addressed to the audience of that historiographic work. DH proclaimed that the rise and fall of Israel's history was a product of national loyalty or disloyalty to God, working in interaction with God's merciful promises. Thus disobedience brought about the fall of Eli's priestly house, but God's promise also produced a new and faithful priestly leadership (1 Sam 2:27-36). In 1 Samuel 12, DH insists that, although choosing kingship had been a serious act of rebellion, God decided to incorporate it into the divine plan. From that point on, the common fate of king and people would depend on whether or not they chose to obey (vv. 14-15, 25). For DH, this strict and unyielding demand for obedience describes the situation for Saul and the later non-Davidic kings of the Northern Kingdom. Their concerted disobedience leads to God's punishment. However, for Judah a new stage is reached in DH when God chooses to reward David's loyal behavior with the promise of a secure and enduring dynasty. Even when disobedient, Davidic kings can always rely on God's steadfast love (2 Sam 7:13-16).

Exilic and postexilic readers of Samuel had experienced radical dislocations in their traditions and institutions. They were living with the consequences of defeat and exile, or later enduring as a people repressed by a powerful world empire. Did the loss of traditional institutions and radical changes in their political and religious life mean that their relationship with God had been shattered? To such an audience, the book of Samuel sought to affirm that God remains faithful even in times of fundamental change. For instance, when the radical new notion of kingship was first adopted, God graciously chose to use it for Israel's good. To be sure, hallowed institutions like the temple of Shiloh and the priesthood of Eli were discarded along the way, but new and better institutions took their place in the form of a more faithful priesthood and the Jerusalem Temple. God's eternal promise to David must have been deeply significant to these exilic and postexilic readers, for whom national independence and native kingship were only fading memories. It pointed those readers to the prospect of a better future under a Davidic king of God's own choosing.

Over the years, Israel's transgressions had endangered its relationship with God, but the case of David the adulterer, murderer, and census taker seeks to encourage despondent readers. God's "mercy is great" (2 Sam 24:14), and God remains willing and able to work around the effects of human disobedience. At the same time, God's implacable punishment of Eli's sons and Saul for intransigent disobedience functions to prevent nonchalant overconfidence (1 Sam 2:25; 3:14; 15:25-29). It remains Israel's responsibility to repent, sacrifice, and return to a life of obedience (2 Sam 12:13-14; 24:10, 17, 25).

A reader today who brings modern political concerns to Samuel may read the book as an exploration of the role of government in human life. The antimonarchical voices in Samuel and those critical of David's behavior point to the state's tendency to institutionalize and intensify the disparity between the powerful and the powerless. Here a modern reader may experience a kinship with ancient Israelite readers who had experienced the tyrannies and apostasies of their kings, beginning with Solomon. Those voices in Samuel that speak out against the excesses of kingship represent an egalitarian ideal found elsewhere in the Old Testament, especially in Deuteronomy and the prophets. These voices insist that centralized power means an unfair concentration of economic resources and leads inevitably to civil violence. Nevertheless, the dominant voice in Samuel speaks a good word for kingship, provided that kingship is established according to God's choice and exercised in obedience to God's will. Centralized power can lead to the evils perpetrated by an apprehensive Saul or an immoral David, but also to the blessings brought by the reign of a repentant and obedient David.[6]

Present-day readers of Samuel may also find themselves fascinated by the dark fate of Saul and the ambiguous character of

David. The tragedy of Saul is suggestive of classic *film noir.* Saul's psychological state, the strengths and defects of his personality, and his conflicted relationship with David intrigue us. We are captivated by the interplay of free will and implacable destiny that leads to his nighttime confrontation with Samuel's ghost and his last stand on Mount Gilboa.

Modern readers can easily identify with David as a person entrapped in moral dilemma and enmeshed with an intensely dysfunctional family. We recognize his faults and offenses in the daily news and in our own lives. We too find ourselves incited by forces beyond our understanding and compelled to make our selections from exclusively bad alternatives (2 Sam 24:1, 12-13). David's dramatic confrontation with Nathan (2 Samuel 12) is likely to have a deep effect on any reader sensitive to its personal implications. The prophet's "You are the one" (v. 7) points a finger out from the page directly at us.

THEMES

Kingship

The Old Testament exhibits contradictory opinions about whether monarchy was ultimately a benefit or a calamity for Israel (contrast Judges 8:23 with Judges 21:25, for example). As we have seen, the book of Samuel presents both promonarchical and antimonarchical views side-by-side. Passages favorable to kingship (1 Sam 9:1–10:16 and 11:1-15) are interwoven with unfavorable ones (8:1-22; 10:17-27; 12:1-25). On the one hand, for Israel to choose kingship and to yearn to be like the nations (8:5, 20) was to reject and despise God (8:7; 10:19). Deciding to adopt monarchy also meant dealing with the grim political realities reflected in the "ways of the king" set forth by 1 Samuel in 8:11-17. Kings do nothing but "take" (the verb is repeated six times). On the other hand, the book also presents the monarchy as a choice in which God proactively participated (10:24-26; 11:6, 13).

Overall, the view presented in Samuel is that kingship was a bad choice for the Israelites to make, but God still chose to remain engaged with them in their insubordinate decision. Consequently the Lord goes ahead and arranges to have Saul anointed as king (1 Sam 8:22; 10:1). Through Samuel, the Lord indicates how Israel may still be God's people even with a king (12:12-15, 20-25). Unfortunately, Saul turns out to be a disobedient failure (13:8-15; 15:1-35). Thus early in Saul's reign, God is already planning on a replacement (13:14; 15:28). However, what the Lord rejects is not kingship itself, but Saul's failure to achieve the potential of kingship (13:13-14; 15:10-11, 35).

The flawed institution of kingship is redeemed by God's willingness to raise up and anoint the "man after [God's] own heart" (13:14). In David, God goes a step beyond Saul and makes a positive investment in kingship in the form of a permanent covenant (2 Sam 7:8-9; 23:5). Under God, the king's proper task is not to enhance his own royal prestige (24:3, 10), but to do God's will for justice (23:3-4). The songs of Hannah and David offer the definitive opinion on kingship, which embraces and interprets whatever else the book of Samuel says on the topic. God "will give strength to his king, / and exalt the power of his anointed" (1 Sam 2:10). God "shows steadfast love to his anointed, / to David and his descendants forever" (2 Sam 22:51).

The Word of God

The word of God is a powerful factor in the unfolding of history. Elkanah's hopeful wish that the Lord's word to Hannah be established (1 Sam 1:23) sets in motion a new beginning for Israel. Israel's story can only be turned in a positive direction when Samuel is called as a trustworthy prophet and the formerly infrequent divine word becomes operative (3:1, 19-21). The words of the prophets come true on a regular basis, forecasting the passing of Eli's priestly family (2:31-36 predicts 4:11 and 22:17-19) and Saul's experience with the spirit (10:2-6 predicts vv. 10-13). As prophet, Samuel transmits divine words of guidance and reproach to the people (8:10; 10:18-19) and to Saul (9:27; 15:2-3, 17-19). The prophets Nathan and Gad censure and advise David with the Lord's word (2 Samuel 7, 12, 24), and David reacts appropriately each time. David regularly seeks oracular guidance (1 Sam 22:10; 23:2, 4; 30:8; 2 Sam 2:1; 5:19, 23). In contrast, Saul rejects God's word (1 Sam 15:23, 26) and finally is faced with the supreme catastrophe of God's unyielding silence (1 Sam 28:6). In the end, David too speaks God's word in the shape of oracles inspired by God's spirit (2 Sam 23:1-2).

House

The frequent repetition of "house" in Samuel provides a unifying factor that binds together disparate material in the book. The word appears more than 160 times, variously signifying "palace," "family," "political unit," and "temple." We read that one priestly house (line of descent) will replace another (1 Sam 2:33, 35). Contrasts and connections are highlighted between the houses of Jonathan and David (1 Sam 20:15-16), Judah and Israel (2 Sam 1:12; 2:4), and Saul and David (3:6). The threat of the sword menaces both the house of Eli (1 Sam 2:33) and the house of David (2 Sam 12:10).

The Nathan oracle of 2 Samuel 7 makes concentrated use of the word. David is settled in his house (palace, v. 1). His wish to build the Lord a house (temple) will only be accomplished by his successor (vv. 2, 5, 6, 7, 13). Instead the Lord will institute a permanent house (dynasty) for David (vv. 11, 16). As the book of Samuel draws to a close, David rejoices in the intimate relationship that exists between his house and God (23:5), but also recognizes the vulnerability of his "father's house" to God's punishment (24:17).

Election

The book of Samuel works to legitimate several of Israel's core institutions by asserting that God elected or chose them. For example, it recounts the priest Eli's lack of perception (1 Sam 1:12-14), the wickedness of his sons (2:12-17, 22-25), and the prediction of an anonymous prophet (2:27-36). These passages work together to legitimate Solomon's later rejection of the family of Eli and his choice of the family of Zadok (1 Kgs 2:27, 35) to serve as Jerusalem's priests. The behavior of the ark indicates that God has chosen Jerusalem as the site of the chief sanctuary, not Shiloh (2 Sam 6:1-15). Moreover, God chose David and his line as the true kings, not Saul and his descendants (6:21; 7:8). God's hidden involvement in the succession to David's throne indicates that God specially elected the royal line of Judah. The story of David's successful altar on the threshing floor outside Jerusalem indicates that God has authorized the site of the Jerusalem Temple (24:18-25). These divine acts of election attest that, although Israel may undergo radical changes and reversals, God's selection of them as a people holds firm (1 Sam 7:23-24; 2 Sam 24:16).

CHAPTER 8

THE BOOKS OF
1 AND 2
KINGS

SHAPES AND STRUCTURES

The title "Kings" reflects both the contents of this book and its core organizing principle. It structures the history of Judah and Israel according to the individual reigns of their kings. These kings are the focal characters, and the fate of each nation hinges on their fidelity or infidelity. However, the prophets also play an important supporting role as adversaries and advisors to the kings and representatives of God's opinions and viewpoint.

Kings falls into three parts. It first recounts the reign of Solomon (1 Kings 1–11), then the parallel stories of Judah and Israel down to the downfall of Israel (1 Kings 12–2 Kings 17), and finally the remainder of Judah's history and its fall (2 Kings 18–25). After Solomon, most kings are dealt with concisely, with only a few sentences supplementing a meager framework. However, a few important kings are treated at greater length.

Between their opening and closing formulas appear more extensive narratives in which prophets usually play important roles. These more significant kings signal critical turning points in the history of Judah and Israel:

• Jeroboam (Israel) and the prophet Ahijah (1 Kings 11–14)
• Ahab (Israel) and Elijah (1 Kings 17–21)
• Jehoram (Israel) and Elisha (2 Kings 3–8)
• Jehu (Israel) and Elisha (2 Kings 9–10)
• Hezekiah (Judah) and Isaiah (2 Kings 18–20)
• Josiah (Judah) and Huldah (2 Kings 22–23)

The most obvious organizing structure is the pattern of opening and closing formulas provided for almost every king. An opening formula matches each king's first year of reign with the term of the monarch of the other kingdom, then states the number of years he reigned. The book describes the entire reign of this one particular king, then turns back to report on the king or kings of the other kingdom who came to the throne during the first king's rule. For example, after describing the forty-one-year reign of Asa king of Judah (1 Kgs 15:9-24), the writer backtracks about forty years to cover the five kings who had succeeded to the throne of Israel during Asa's reign (15:25–22:40). This reciprocating and synchronizing movement has the effect of bringing together the histories of two separate kingdoms into the story of a single people.

The opening formulas always judge the kings of Israel negatively. They did "evil in the sight of the LORD" by offering sacrifice outside Jerusalem in defiance of the law of Deuteronomy 12. Certain kings of Judah are also criticized, and others receive only limited approval because they permitted worship outside Jerusalem at the local "high places." Unqualified endorsement is reserved only for Hezekiah and Josiah, because they limited sacrifice to the Jerusalem Temple. The closing formulas refer to sources used by the writer and report on the king's death and his successor. Additional information is furnished for the kings of Judah, such as their age at accession and mother's name. These introductions and conclusions vary in wording, but become more fixed for the last rulers of each kingdom. Significantly, two events take place outside this framework. One is the unobserved transfer of prophetic authority from Elijah to Elisha (2 Kings 2). The other is the illegitimate regime of Queen Athaliah in Judah (2 Kings 11).[1]

A repeated pattern of prophetic promises and their fulfillment furnishes a further system of organization. The prophets are the Lord's servants, announcing divine will and judgment (2 Kgs 17:13, 23; 21:10; 24:2). The proclamation and subsequent fulfillment of their words unify the book of Kings and provide it with structure. Instances of this prediction and fulfillment pattern are:

- the partition of the united kingdom (1 Kgs 11:29-39; 12:15)
- the fall of Israel (1 Kgs 14:15-16; 2 Kgs 17:23)
- the fate of Omri's dynasty (1 Kgs 21:21-24; 2 Kgs 9:7-10; 10:17)
- the overthrow of Judah (2 Kgs 21:10-15; 22:15-17; 24:2).

The most striking case is a precise prediction of Josiah's reform made three hundred years beforehand (1 Kgs 13:1-3; 2 Kgs 23:15-18).

Parallels between similar narratives provide another sort of correlation. Examples are:

- two mothers and their sons (1 Kgs 3:16-28; 2 Kgs 6:26-31)
- death of the wicked queen (2 Kgs 9:30-37; 11:13-16)
- God appears to Solomon (1 Kgs 3:4-15; 9:1-9)
- wisdom or folly with visitors (1 Kgs 10:1-13; 2 Kgs 20:12-19)
- a son dies (1 Kgs 14:1-18; 17:17-24)
- a son comes back to life (1 Kgs 17:17-24; 2 Kgs 4:18-37).

In addition, evaluative discourses appear at two important turning points in the narrative. These review the past and point forward to the challenges of the future. The first is Solomon's upbeat prayer at the temple dedication (1 Kings 8). The second is a disapproving editorial statement about the cause of Israel's downfall (2 Kings 17).

ISSUES IN READING

The author of Kings was the Deuteronomistic Historian (DH; see chap. 4). DH used older sources and cited three of these by name. The "Book of the Acts of Solomon" reported on Solomon's deeds and his "wisdom" (1 Kgs 11:41). This source provided administrative lists and other historical notes. It also contained legendary anecdotes illustrating Solomon's glory and wisdom. Data about the later kings was culled from two other sources. These are called the "Book of the Annals of the Kings of Israel" and the "Book of the Annals of the Kings of Judah" (1 Kgs 14:19, 29). These two works included particulars about each king's wars and building projects, as well as conspiracies they faced (1 Kgs 14:19, 30; 15:23, 32; 16:20; 22:39, 45; 2 Kgs 20:20). Because the author assumed that these works were accessible to readers, they apparently were not official annals. Rather they appear to have been literary works, perhaps dependent on inscriptions and other reliable sources. In addition, DH employed the conclusion of the Throne Succession Story (see chap. 7) to describe the accession of Solomon (1 Kings 1–2).

Much of the rest of the book derives from prophetic source materials. Previously collected stories about Elijah and Elisha make up nearly all of 1 Kings 17:1 to 2 Kings 8:15. The story cycles of these two prophets are held together by the transfer of Elijah's mantle to Elisha (2 Kgs 2:13-14) and the eventual completion of his mission (1 Kgs 19:15-17). For this reason, scholars usually assume that these stories had already been gathered into a unified whole before being taken up and used by DH. Narratives about other prophets (Ahijah, 1 Kgs 11:29-39; 14:1-18; Shemaiah, 1 Kgs 12:21-24; Micaiah, 1 Kgs 22:1-28) presumably also go back to earlier prophetic sources of some kind. Of these, the stories about Isaiah are the most extensive and independent (2 Kgs 18:13–20:19).

The reliability of Kings as a historical source has been the subject of much scholarly discussion. Its use of sources indicates that it has considerable historical value in places. Archaeology and other external sources sometimes show Kings to be correct about matters ranging from the name of the king of Moab (2 Kgs 3:4) to King Hezekiah's construction of a water tunnel (2 Kgs 20:20). In contrast, the source used to reconstruct the reign of Solomon seems to have mixed trustworthy historical data (such as a list of the administrative districts of the kingdom, 1 Kgs 4:7-19) with folktales celebrating Solomon's wealth and wisdom.

Although the author used sources in a way somewhat similar to the practice of modern historians, the theory of historical causation in Kings is theological rather than political or economic.

For example, the short shrift given to the important northern king Omri (1 Kgs 16:23-28) manifests a controlling interest in theology that excludes more mundane concerns. In a similar way, the author seems to have vilified the reputation of the Baal-worshiping kings Ahab and his son Jehoram by twisting some historical circumstances. Kings has them engaging in a series of wars in which Syria dominated Israel (1 Kings chaps. 20 and 22; 2 Kgs 6:8–7:20; 8:7-15). However, it is likely that these wars actually took place in a later period when Israel was weaker.

Many of the narratives in Kings, especially the folktales and stories about the prophets, cannot be used as trustworthy historical sources. For example, it is difficult to reconcile the optimistic story of God's miraculous rescue of Jerusalem from the attack of the Assyrian king Sennacherib (esp. 2 Kgs 19:35-37) with the picture presented in Sennacherib's own annals. The Assyrian sources make it clear that, even though Jerusalem was not actually captured, Judah had to pay a huge tribute and lost a good deal of its territory.

The chronology used to date the kings' reigns is also questionable. The years of reign given for the kings of Israel do not coordinate internally with those for the kings of Judah. Moreover, the cross dating between the two kingdoms does not always match up with the reign lengths given for the various kings. Sometimes the dates indicated in Kings do not agree with well-established dates from Mesopotamian sources.

THE PLOT OF KINGS

Kings consists of a series of individual narratives set into a chronological framework. These narratives may be as short as a sentence or two portraying some event of historical interest (such as 1 Kgs 14:25-28), or a more complex account extending to several chapters (for example 2 Kings 18–19). The chronological framework unites these diversified narratives into a coherent plot movement. It transforms an assortment of disconnected narratives about royal deeds and prophetic words and acts into a united narrative about the fate of the two kingdoms of Israel and Judah.

Of course, there is no real suspense about the outcome of this plot, for even the earliest readers already knew that both kingdoms would be destroyed in the end. Nevertheless, Kings speaks about the final ending with ambiguity, telling the story "as though" Israel and Judah had a prospect of obeying and surviving. It invites the reader to "play along" and suppose that the outcome could be in doubt. Thus unequivocal predictions of the fall of the Northern Kingdom like that of 1 Kings 14:15-16 are followed by repeated statements of the Lord's continuing leniency and pardon, such as 2 Kings 13:4-5 and 14:26-27. The Lord repeatedly sends prophets to give warnings. Even though all the kings of Israel do evil without a single exception, there are some positive aspects about the behavior of Jehu, Jehoahaz, and even Israel's last king, Hoshea (2 Kgs 10:18-28; 13:4; 17:2).

The story of Judah is told with even more ambivalence and openness to the possibility of a happy ending. The behavior of Judah's kings is mixed. Some do evil, many are partially obedient, and a few are godly reformers. Furthermore, the survival of Judah at times appears to be absolutely guaranteed by God's promise to the family of David that they would always rule in Jerusalem. For this reason, the reader may encounter the ending of Kings as a wrenching surprise. Royal behavior reaches the height of obedience with Hezekiah (2 Kings 18–20), followed immediately by the low point of Manasseh's idolatrous misdeeds (chap. 21). At this point Judah's inescapable death sentence is announced (2 Kgs 21:10-15). Even so, the reader might reasonably assume there is still hope, for Josiah then appears (chaps. 22–23). His reform of the people's religious life fulfills every expectation of obedience and virtue. Yet the shocking oracle he receives from the prophet Huldah makes it clear that Judah is nevertheless doomed (22:16-17). In spite of God's promise to David and in spite of Josiah's willingness to correct all Judah's violations of divine law, Judah's last four kings preside over a rapid slide into national catastrophe (23:31–25:21).

One might imagine the plot lines for these separate kingdoms as two trajectories under the influence of three competing gravitational forces: the obedience and disobedience of the kings, the prophetic word, and God's gracious patience. In the case of the Northern Kingdom Israel, their constant transgression and refusal to listen to the prophets (2 Kgs 17:14, 40; 18:12) produced a relatively straight downward path into disaster. In the case of Judah, however, another force enters the equation: the Lord's eternal promise to David's descendants. As a result, Judah's trajectory is more complex. Judah's kings tend to listen to the prophets who warn or advise them (e.g., 1 Kgs 12:24; 22:5, 7). Some kings are obedient, and several act as religious reformers (Hezekiah and Josiah). The promise to David is invoked three times to explain Judah's continued security (1 Kgs 11:36; 15:4; 2 Kgs 8:19). Nevertheless, in the end Judah too crashes to the ground, forced down by Manasseh's intransigent sin (2 Kgs 23:26-27; 24:2-4) and Judah's arousal of the Lord's anger (22:13, 17; 21:6, 15; 24:20). Finally, Israel and Judah share the same fate. Compare the parallel passages, 2 Kings 17:23*b* and 25:21*b*. Whether or not Kings points beyond this final catastrophe to some future hope for Judah or for the Davidic kings is a matter of scholarly controversy.

The shape of the plot of Kings may be thought of as an exploration of the nation's disobedience and resulting doom presented in three acts. Act I (1 Kings 1–11) focuses on the united kingdom of Solomon. The action rises from the commencement of Solomon's reign through his pious wisdom, temple building, and prosperity, and then abruptly falls into idolatry and rebellion. Act II (1 Kings 12–2 Kings 17) is presented on a "split screen," alternating between the story of the northern kingdom and that of Judah. The picture for the kingdom of Judah has high points and low points regarding obedience and national success, but it is always sustained by the unchanging "safety net" of God's promise to David. Indeed, the rhythm of Judah's history reflects the pattern of David's biography as presented in Samuel. In contrast, the story of the Northern Kingdom is more like the story of Saul. Things start bad and get worse. In the end, the kingdom of Israel commits national suicide. This double focus is replaced by a return to a single focus in Act III (2 Kings 18–24), for the only story left to tell is that of Judah. An interchange of hero kings (Hezekiah, Josiah) and villain kings (Manasseh, Josiah's four successors) in turn offers the reader alternating hope and despair about Judah's destiny. The last scene is one of defeat and exile (2 Kgs 25:1-26), with only the slightest hint of hope for a positive tomorrow (25:27-30).[2]

Act I: Solomon in Glory and Dishonor (1 Kings 1–11)

The material about Solomon introduces many of the themes of Kings. Solomon's example of obedience and disobedience sets up the positive and negative possibilities of the nation's future. His construction of the Temple (1 Kings 6–8) makes it possible for Israel to obey for the first time the law of Deuteronomy 12 mandating the centralization of all sacrifice in one place. Moreover, the word of the prophet Ahijah announces the Lord's unconditional promise to David's descendants (1 Kgs 11:31-39).

After an account of his accession (1 Kings 1–2), the career of Solomon is reported positively (chaps. 3–10) under the themes of wisdom, royal power, building programs, and piety. The story of Kings begins not in power but in weakness and disorder. David is old and impotent (1:1-4), not able to "know" either his new concubine or the court intrigue that is taking place around him (vv. 11, 18). The rival supporters of David's two sons Adonijah and Solomon engage in stratagems of dubious integrity to put their favored candidate on the throne. Adonijah hosts a suspicious gathering (vv. 9-10). However, Nathan tells what seems to be an outright lie in Solomon's behalf (v. 11). He and Solomon's mother, Bathsheba, put the worst possible construction on Adonijah's behavior (vv. 18-19, 24-26). They convince the old king that he has made a promise he may never have uttered (vv. 13, 17, 30; such a promise is not recorded elsewhere), and Solomon is enthroned on the basis of this tawdry intrigue. When David dies, Solomon enacts a bloody purge against potential troublemakers (2:13-46), so that "the kingdom was established in the hand of Solomon" (v. 46, cf. v. 12).

This is more than just a report of a successful court intrigue, however, for it launches concepts that continue to drive the plot of Kings. The Lord is behind the events of history and has brought Solomon to the throne (1 Kgs 1:48 according to David; 2:24 according to Solomon). David's last words to Solomon outline the goal God has in mind for all succeeding reigns: Kings who obey God's law will prosper (2:2-3). The central question of the plot of Kings is whether these high expectations will be realized in the kings who follow.

At first Solomon's reign seems like a golden age, and there are high hopes for it (1 Kgs 1:37, 47). Solomon intends that lasting peace should follow from his initial violence (2:33, 45). He exercises God-given wisdom in all things (3:16-28; 4:29-34; 10:1-13). Both Solomon and his subjects enjoy peace and prosperity (4:1-28, esp. 24-25; 9:15-28; 10:14-29). The centerpiece of his accomplishments is the construction of the temple. This fulfillment of God's promise to David has been made possible by the "rest" God granted Solomon from all enemies (5:4-5; 8:15-21). The legitimacy of the Jerusalem Temple is emphasized by the presence of the ark and God's glory (8:1-13). Solomon's lengthy dedication prayer stresses its vital importance as a place of supplication (8:22-53). God has chosen it forever (9:3).

Again, however, the reader is pointed firmly toward questions about future events. In spite of all the hope expressed here (1 Kgs 8:66), the future still depends on obedience. God has promised to remain connected to the temple and to Israel if Solomon and the people remain obedient (6:11-13; 8:56-61). But will he and his successors practice God's law? The temple now makes it possible for Israel's kings to obey the law of Deuteronomy 12 by centralizing all sacrifice (contrast 3:3). Will they do so, or will they let the local shrines continue to operate? The reader is notified that the future is in doubt, for Solomon's prayer hints that defeat and exile may lie ahead (8:46-50). Moreover, God threatens plainly that disobedience and worship of other gods could lead to subjugation and the destruction of the temple (9:6-9).

There is a more immediate threat in the short term. Solomon rules over two political entities, Israel and Judah (1 Kgs 1:35). Solomon thus sits "on the throne of Israel" (8:20). According to David (2:4), God had promised that this situation of a united monarchy would continue only if Solomon and his successors were to be obedient and loyal to God. Then and only then would David's descendants continue to rule "on the throne of Israel," enjoying dominion over the Northern Kingdom as well as over Judah. Solomon repeats this conditional promise about the throne of Israel in 8:25, and God restates it in an appearance to Solomon after the temple is completed (9:4-5). Obedience will lead to the establishment of Solomon's "royal throne over Israel forever." However, the reader will soon discover that this is not to be.

In 1 Kings 11, the portrayal of Solomon turns negative. He is enticed by foreign wives into the worship of alien gods and threatened by adversaries, including a domestic rebellion by Jeroboam (v. 26). The Lord predicts a partial success for this rebellion directly to Solomon (vv. 11-13) and to Jeroboam by means of the prophet Ahijah (vv. 29-39). The kingdom is to be torn apart and divided between Jeroboam and Solomon's heir. The conditional divine promise of 2:4; 8:25; 9:4-5 will not be kept. Solomon's offspring will not occupy the "throne of Israel." However, because of David's extraordinary obedience, God does vow unconditionally that his family will reign over Judah forever (11:32, 34-36). Again, the reader is directed to think about the future. On the one hand, God pledges to Jeroboam an enduring dynasty "over Israel" if Jeroboam can be as obedient as David was (vv. 37-38). On the other, the punishment to be suffered by David's offspring is "not forever" (v. 39), and their future remains open to new developments.

The presentation of Solomon's reign introduces pivotal tensions and problems that drive the ensuing plot of Kings. First, Solomon's initial uprightness (1 Kgs 3:3) and subsequent turn to do "evil in the sight of the LORD" (11:6) initiates the criterion of judgment that will be applied to each king who follows. Did he do what was right or what was evil? Second, Solomon's apostasy with foreign gods (11:1-8) will be repeated again and again by the kings of both north and south, until it is specifically undone by Josiah's reformation (2 Kgs 23:10, 13). Third, Solomon's construction of the temple introduces a new prospect for sin. Although Solomon's temple makes it possible for the first time to obey the law mandating the centralization of sacrifices (Deuteronomy 12), paradoxically it also means that disobedience is now possible. Sacrifice to the Lord outside Jerusalem will soon begin (12:26-33), inaugurating the nation's other great act of apostasy. This will also continue until the reform of Josiah (2 Kgs 23:8-9, 15-20).

In Kings, the Lord never does anything significant without providing a prophetic warning (2 Kgs 17:13, 23; 21:10-15; 24:2). Ahijah first introduces the concept of the prophetic word to the plot. This word will regularly reappear to spell out royal sin (as in 11:11-13) and God's emerging plan (as in vv. 31-39). Ahijah also restates the Lord's promise to David of eternal rule in Jerusalem (11:36). The unfolding plot of Kings will show whether God will choose to keep this promise (15:14; 2 Kgs 8:19), or perhaps discard it (2 Kgs 25:27-30).

Act II: The Stories of Israel and Judah (1 Kings 12–2 Kings 17)

Scene 1: The Effects of Folly and Sin (1 Kings 12–16). The concluding events of Solomon's reign lead to parallel stories of folly on the part of Solomon's successor Rehoboam (1 Kgs 12:1-19) and of outrageous sin on the part of Jeroboam (12:25-33). Rehoboam's folly brings about a division into two kingdoms (vv. 16, 19), leading to the separate but interrelated plot strands that follow and to recurring hostility between the newly independent kingdoms. Solomon's labor policies had planted the seeds of this national discord (5:13; 11:28), but this partition of the nation also results from the Lord's activity in the arena of history and the fulfillment of a prophetic word (12:15, 22-24). The conditional promise of the "throne of Israel" (2:4; 8:25; 9:4-5) is nullified.

The parallel story of the sin of Jeroboam has both short-term and long-term effects. His most heinous transgression was to set up an alternative place of sacrifice outside Jerusalem in violation of Deuteronomy 12 (1 Kgs 12:27-28), but he offends in other ways as well (12:32-33; 13:33). Two examples of prophetic word are directed at Jeroboam's sin. The first word, delivered against Jeroboam's altar (13:2-3), points the reader forward in expectation to the birth and reforms of King Josiah. Perhaps this suggests to the reader that the story told by Kings might conceivably have a happy ending in the long run, at least for the kingdom of Judah. However, a second prophetic word, delivered by way of Jeroboam's wife, prepares for negative consequences (14:7-16). Jeroboam's behavior has not been like David's (vv. 7-9) and so he has lost the opportunity to found a dynasty like David's, as the Lord had conditionally promised (11:38). His house will succumb (13:34; 14:10-14). More seriously, the sin of Jeroboam has done permanent damage to Israel's relationship with God, and the Northern Kingdom is already doomed to defeat and exile (14:15-16). From a literary standpoint, the result is that there is really no suspense in the plot of the Northern Kingdom. It is doomed, and it is only a question of how long this doom can be delayed and what shape it will take. However, the parallel story of Judah remains uncertain. If the Northern Kingdom slides into inevitable disaster, the story of Judah will reflect drama and suspense, having its ups and downs before the final resolution is reached.

First Kings 14:21–16:34 digests about fifty years of history to illustrate the effects of Rehoboam's folly and Jeroboam's transgression. The plot thread for Judah entails the royal crime of permitting sacrifice outside Jerusalem at high places (14:22-24;

15:3). However, this is mitigated by partial reform efforts (15:12-13, contrast v. 14) and the Lord's willingness to stand by the unconditional promise to David's house (15:4). The corresponding Northern Kingdom plot line reflects only evil as kings "walk in the way of Jeroboam" (15:26, 34; 16:19, 26). The consequences for both kingdoms are brutal: invasion, civil war, conspiracies, and the destruction of short-lived dynasties. Once more the prophetic word is active (15:29-30; 16:2-4, 7). The situation of the Northern Kingdom finally hits bottom with King Ahab, whose apostasy transcends anything that has come before (16:30). Ahab and his pagan wife Jezebel go beyond Jeroboam's sin of sacrificing to the Lord outside Jerusalem and initiate a state-sponsored worship of Baal (vv. 31-33).

Scene 2: Israel and the Prophets (1 Kings 17–2 Kings 8). Now the focus shifts from kings to prophets. These narratives concentrate on Elijah and Elisha, exploring their conflict with the apostate kings of Ahab's family. The plot reflects a conflict between the Lord and Baal and between life and death. The Lord wins a public contest with Baal on Mount Carmel (1 Kgs 18:20-40). Moreover, the Lord as the God of life is victorious over all those powers that stand against life. By means of the prophets Elijah and Elisha, God overpowers drought (1 Kgs 18:41-46), hunger (1 Kgs 17:8-16; 19:4-8; 2 Kgs 4:42-44; 7:1-20), thirst (2 Kgs 2:19-22), debt (2 Kgs 4:1-7), infertility (2 Kgs 4:11-17), disease (2 Kgs 5:1-19), and even death itself (1 Kgs 17:17-24; 2 Kgs 4:18-37). These two prophets confront Ahab and his successors with the consequences of the disbelief and disobedience they exhibit in the practice of war (1 Kgs 20:31-43; 22:1-40), in the injustices they commit (1 Kings 21), and in their apostate religious practices (2 Kings 1).[3]

The Lord remains an active player in the unfolding plot, at times giving victory and protection to the people (2 Kgs 3:4-27; 6:8-23) and keeping the dynastic promise made to David (2 Kgs 8:19). God's commission to Elijah (1 Kgs 19:15-17) organizes and drives the plot of this section. The assignment to anoint Hazael as a new king in Damascus and Jehu as a reforming king over the Northern Kingdom are fulfilled in due time by his successor Elisha (2 Kgs 8:7-15 and 9:1-13).

Scene 3: Revolution and Reformation (2 Kings 9–12). In this scene, attention returns from an exclusive focus on the Northern Kingdom back to a split-screen presentation of both kingdoms.

The reader encounters parallel stories about mirror-image reforms and their results. Jehu's conspiracy and unavailing reform in the Northern Kingdom provide a negative counterpart for a successful coup d'état and reform in Judah.

The story of Jehu (2 Kings 9–10) begins on a hopeful note. His revolution is prophetically inspired. He is anointed by the Lord's command in the same way David had been (9:6), and he wipes out the entire house of Ahab to fulfill the Lord's word (9:7-10, 24-26, 36-37; 10:10, 17). He suppresses the worship of Baal. In the end, his zeal (10:16) wins him a dynasty "on the throne of Israel" that lasts for several generations (v. 30).[4] Ultimately, however, Jehu's continued adherence to the religious policies of Jeroboam (vv. 29, 31) means that the overall situation is no better, and Israel's territory is accordingly reduced (vv. 32-33).

The revolution in Judah led by the priest Jehoiada and the subsequent reform of King Joash (2 Kings 11–12) offer a less violent and more successful parallel to Jehu's actions. The two episodes correspond in several ways. In each an evil queen mother is killed (9:30-37; 11:13-16) and a temple of Baal is destroyed (10:26-27; 11:18). The prophetic word in one case and priestly office in the other legitimate the revolutions. In each, trumpets and popular acclamation accompany royal anointing (9:12-13; 11:12, 14). Ultimately though, the Syrian king Hazael threatens each kingdom (10:32-33; 12:17-18).

However, whereas Jehu's reformation is fruitless, the one in Judah is fruitful. It restores all that is proper (2 Kgs 11:14, "according to custom") and legitimate. Most important, instead of founding a new dynasty, the revolution in Judah restores the proper Davidic one. The reign of Queen Athaliah was doubly illegitimate. Not only was she a member of the apostate family of Ahab (2 Kgs 8:26-27), but she was not descended from David. In order to make her illegitimacy clear to the reader, chapter 11 is reported outside the system of paralleled reigns.[5] The reforming actions of making a covenant (11:17) and restructuring temple procedures (12:4-16) point to the future. They foreshadow the accomplishments of the outstanding reformer Josiah (cf. 11:17 with 23:3 and 12:4-16 with 22:4-7). Nevertheless, Judah's position remains ambiguous. Joash must buy off Hazael (with temple assets!) and in the end is assassinated. Furthermore, the high places are not removed (12:3).

Scene 4: Israel Slides into Disaster (2 Kings 13–17). The parallel stories of Judah and Israel now move into "fast-forward" as 2 Kings 13–15 quickly covers several decades. Yet the circumstances of the Northern Kingdom do not decline precipitously or overnight. Although there is sin and defeat, the Lord nevertheless remains engaged and protective (13:4-5, 23; 14:26-27). The reader is given to understand that the blame for the final tragic outcome cannot be attributed to the Lord. Yet Israel's state becomes increasingly desperate through chapter 15. King Menahem of Israel must pay the Assyrian king a huge tribute (vv. 19-20). The story of Judah also remains ambiguous and uncertain, with incomplete piety and mixed successes. King Ahaz of Judah is a particularly ambiguous figure, committing depraved apostasies (16:2-4), but also building the Lord a new altar.[6] He suffers reverses and is obliged to pay tribute to Assyria.

Final catastrophe strikes the Northern Kingdom when the Assyrians crush the nation and exile its people. Of course, Israel's fate comes as no surprise to the reader, although even here there is a certain ambiguity. Israel's last king, Hoshea, is not as bad as his predecessors have been (2 Kgs 17:2), but doom overwhelms the nation anyway. In 17:7-41, the author editorializes on the reasons for the fall of Israel. All the past faults of the Northern Kingdom are made abundantly clear (vv. 7-18, 21-23). Moreover, the newly imported settlers in the north behave no better (vv. 24-41). This accusatory harangue directs reader interest both backward to explain Israel's fate and forward to forecast Judah's behavior and future (vv. 19-20). The prophetic warnings (vv. 13, 23) have come to Judah as well as to Israel, and the Lord's anger (vv. 11, 17) will strike out against Judah too (21:6, 15; 23:19, 26; 24:20). The reader will soon see that Israel's refusal to listen (2 Kgs 17:14, 40) will also be typical of Judah (21:9). Judah will also imitate the Northern Kingdom's devotion to idols (17:12, 15; 21:11, 21; 23:24) and its worship of other gods (17:7, 35-38; 22:17). As the story of the north ends, all attention turns to focus on Judah, which now stands alone to work out its fate.

Act III: Judah Stands Alone and Falls (2 Kings 18–25)

Scene 1: Disobedience and Reform (2 Kings 18–23). In spite of what has been said in 2 Kings 17:19-20, Judah's doom does not

yet appear to be completely sealed, at least to the hopeful reader. The prevailing wickedness of its kings remains counterbal-
anced by the Lord's unambiguous promise to David. The
remaining story of Judah falls into a pattern of alternating righteous and wicked kings: Hezekiah (chaps. 18–20), Manasseh (21),
Josiah (22–23), and Josiah's successors (24–25). The book's climax will come with Josiah, but first the reader is presented with
contrasting models of kingship: Hezekiah, the best king since
David (18:3-6), and Manasseh, absolutely the worst king Judah
ever had.

Hezekiah's rectitude is manifested by his success even against
the invincible Assyrians (2 Kgs 18:13–19:37) and his piety in the
face of mortal illness (20:1-11). Yet the deep ambiguity of Judah's
ultimate fate continues to be an issue. The Lord's miraculous
deliverance of Jerusalem from Assyria stands in marked contrast
to Isaiah's prediction of an impending triumphant invasion by
Babylon (20:12-19). Manasseh is Hezekiah's opposite in every
way, reversing his father's obedient religious policies (21:2-9),
provoking the Lord's wrath (v. 15), and instigating evil in the
whole people (v. 16). Now Judah's doom appears to be irre-
versible (vv. 10-15).

In due time Manasseh is succeeded by his grandson Josiah,
whose reform climaxes the entire book of Kings. The catalyst for
his reform is a rediscovery of the book of God's law (2 Kgs 22:3-
11), a document similar to the present book of Deuteronomy. The
unfulfilled demands of this law endanger the nation with the
Lord's wrath (22:13). The prophet Huldah soon makes it clear to
both Josiah and the reader that nothing will be able to avert this
divine anger (vv. 16-17). Nevertheless, Josiah faithfully goes
ahead and makes a covenant with the whole people in a renewed
commitment to obedience (23:1-3). He extends reform both to
Judah (vv. 4-14) and into territory in the former kingdom of Israel
(vv. 15-20). Even though Josiah's reform makes no difference
whatsoever in the Lord's determination to punish Judah (vv. 26-
27), it is still deeply satisfying for the reader. Readers are likely to
admire Josiah's willingness to obey the law without any hope of
reward or any motive of earning God's favor. Moreover, so many
of the unresolved plot themes of Kings are settled at this point
that Josiah's reformation must be understood as the true climax
of the plot of Kings.

• According to the law book's requirements, Josiah eliminates all the "high places" where sacrifice outside Jerusalem had been practiced (23:8-9). Generations of Judah's kings had left these untouched.

• Josiah resolves another long-standing plot tension by explicitly undoing the "sin of Jeroboam" at Bethel. His demolition of the Bethel altar (vv. 15-18) finally fulfills a prophecy announced back in 1 Kings 13:2.

• He eliminates apostate worship practices that go back as far as Solomon (23:13-14).

• He obliterates the more recent sinful innovations of the kings of Judah and especially Manasseh (vv. 5-7, 10-12).

However, plots do not just unfold or thicken; sometimes they twist, and the plot of Kings twists abruptly at this point. Josiah's unexplained and mysterious death at the hand of Pharaoh Neco (2 Kgs 23:29) comes as a jarring shock to the reader, who certainly expects something quite different in view of Huldah's prophecy (22:18-20).[7]

Scene 2: Destruction and Exile (2 Kings 24–25). Briefer reports sketch the wickedness and rebellions of Josiah's four successors. Behind the maneuvers of Israel, Egypt, and Babylon, the real actor remains the Lord, who acts out of anger to fulfill the prophetic word and punish the sin of Manasseh (2 Kgs 24:2-4, 20). Almost every item of Judah's national culture is undone: kingship, temple, city, priesthood, and leadership (25:7, 10, 13-21). In a sense, even the exodus itself is reversed as some of the people return to Egypt (v. 26).

Kings ends with an ambiguous report about King Jehoiachin as an honored captive in Babylon until his death (2 Kgs 25:27-30). This has been interpreted both positively as a sign of a potential future for the Davidic dynasty and negatively as the decisive last act in the national tragedy. Is the king's honorable captivity until death a hollow favor that only emphasizes the hopelessness of Judah's situation? After all, the most that Kings ever actually promises exiles is an improvement of their lives in captivity (1 Kgs 8:46-50). Alternatively, is this paragraph a quiet signal that it is at least possible that the Lord might still prove willing to act for the good of the defeated and exiled people? After all, the promises to David of an unending reign have not been repudiated, and the slender hint of national reunification from 1 Kings

11:39 still hangs suspended in mid-air. Perhaps it is best simply to read this as an indication that Judah's future is open and depends entirely on whatever God may choose to do.

CONTEXTS AND AUDIENCES

Even before the book of Kings was written, its component narratives functioned as commentaries on the role of prophets and the behavior of kings. Stories about the prophets make up a substantial portion of Kings. These prophetic narratives were originally passed on by word of mouth in order to uphold the office of prophet and the power of the prophetic word. The prophet was presented as an exemplary figure to be followed (1 Kgs 19:20-21). The prophet was held up as someone to be respected (2 Kgs 8:3-6), obeyed (1 Kgs 17:10-16; 2 Kgs 5:10-14), or perhaps even feared (2 Kgs 1:9-15; 2:23-24). These stories recounting the power of a prophet's word or deed were told to instill a sense of awe and wonder in those who heard them (2 Kgs 2:19-22; 4:38-41, 42-44). Later some of these prophetic stories were collected and written down into a cycle of tales about Elijah and Elisha (1 Kgs 17:1–2 Kgs 8:15). In this form they served as a negative commentary on the apostate policies of Ahab and his successors and a positive assertion of the Lord's power to bring life in the midst of death and to defeat Israel's enemies. A briefer collection of tales about Isaiah supported the notion that the Lord specially protected Jerusalem from outside attack and highlighted the power of the prophetic word (2 Kgs 18:13–20:19). The context for these collections appears to have been the late monarchy periods of Israel and Judah respectively.

The historical situation of the audience of the original written form of Kings is hotly debated. Some suggest that the book was first composed as an optimistic work, written in the late preexilic period. Because Huldah's prediction of Josiah's peaceful end (2 Kgs 22:20) contradicts his actual violent demise (23:29), most have suggested that the book was composed before his death. However, the introduction to Josiah in 22:1 mentions the total length of his reign, which implies a date of composition immediately after the traumatic death of the great reformer. In either case, Kings, as part of the larger Deuteronomistic History, would have been intended to generate support for a continuation of Josiah's reforming policies. After the fall of Judah, the historical context changed radically, and the book's original theological point no longer applied. In the exile, therefore, Kings was revised in a more pessimistic direction into a history of disobedience that blamed the nation's fall on the sins of Manasseh (21:10-15; 23:26-27; 24:3-4).

Other scholars believe that the first form of Kings was not produced until after the death of Judah's last king Jehoiachin (2 Kgs 25:27-30). If this is true, then the initial audience would have been readers who had recently experienced Judah's defeat and exile. One can get an impression of the baffled, angry, and dismal mood of this audience by reading Psalms 79 and 137. After the collapse of Judah, traumatized Jews lived scattered in Palestine, Egypt, and Babylon. Lamentations witnesses to the state of those remaining in Palestine: hunger (Lam 1:11, 19; 2:19-20), overturned social structures (4:5; 5:8, 12), ruin of the temple (1:10; 2:7), foreign control of the land and its resources (5:2, 4). Jeremiah reports the cynical attitude of many exiles in Egypt who abandoned loyalty to the Lord (Jer 44:8-10, 15-19). Ezekiel reports the despair of those in Babylon: "How then can we live?" (Ezek 33:10); "we are cut off completely" (37:11). Many protested that God had been unjust: "The way of the Lord is unfair" (Ezek 18:25). Our ancestors did the sinning, but we have borne the punishment (Ezek 18:2; Lam 5:7). To an audience reading the book of Kings (and the rest of the Deuteronomistic History) after the fall of Judah, it would serve as a rationale for the doom they had just experienced. God's judgment was inevitable and just, given their long history of defiance and disbelief (1 Kgs 9:6-9; 2 Kgs 17:7-41). The best thing they can do now is repent (1 Kgs 8:46-53) and hope for the best.[8]

THEMES

Apostasy and Reform

On the basis of the tenets of Deuteronomy, Kings keeps up a steady critique of the nation's failure to preserve the purity and unity of its worship. For example, the charges leveled against Rehoboam and Ahaz (1 Kgs 14:22-24; 2 Kgs 16:3-4) directly allude to what is forbidden by Deuteronomy 12:2-3, 29-31. One focus of criticism is the worship of foreign gods. This practice starts with Solomon and is continued by various kings of Israel and Judah. The worship of other gods is sometimes called the "way of the kings of Israel" (2 Kgs 8:18; 16:3) or "of the house of Ahab" (2 Kgs 8:27). The book of Kings particularly disdains the worship of Baal. Baal religion is championed by Ahab and Jezebel (1 Kgs 16:31-32), purged by Jehu in Israel (2 Kgs 10:18-28) and by those loyal to Joash in Judah (11:18), but then revived again by Manasseh (21:3). Josiah finally eliminates it in Jerusalem (23:4-5).

A second focal point of censure is sacrifice outside the Jerusalem Temple. Deuteronomy 12 forbids any noncentral sacrifice. Because they sacrificed at Bethel, all the northern kings are automatically condemned for participating in the "way" or "sins of Jeroboam" (1 Kgs 15:34; 16:2, 19, 26, 31; etc.). Noncentral sacrifice also took place at local "high places" in Judah. Several otherwise conscientious kings of Judah receive only qualified approval because "the high places were not taken away" (e.g., 1 Kgs 15:14; 22:43). Kings reserves unconditional praise only for Hezekiah and Josiah, who finally shut down these high places.

The two strands of "other gods" and "sacrifice outside Jerusalem" are brought together in the reform of Josiah. He eliminates both alien cults (2 Kgs 23:4-5, 10-14) and local high places (23:8-9) in Judah. He also desecrates the shrine of Bethel and the other high places of Israel (23:15-20). The infidelity of the Northern Kingdom has led to its destruction by Assyria (2 Kgs 17:7-18, 21-23), and Judah, inspite of Josiah, will fall to Babylon because of similar offenses (vv. 19-20), especially those sponsored by Manasseh (2 Kgs 21:10-15; 24:3-4).

Consequently, Kings features a plot rhythm of repeated apostasy and reform, comparable in some ways to the structure of the book of Judges. Solomon's unfaithfulness lays the groundwork for the transgression of both Jeroboam (Israel) and Rehoboam (Judah). Ahab (Israel) establishes a negative model for his relatives in both north and south, while Asa (Judah) provides a contrasting example of obedience. Jehu (Israel) and Joash (Judah) are contemporary reformers. The story of Judah climaxes with the extreme contrast between the wicked Manasseh and his righteous predecessor Hezekiah and successor Josiah. In the end, though, Josiah's perfect reformation makes no difference in God's implacable decision to punish Judah for Manasseh's sins.

Davidic Kingship

Another important theme is God's special favor to David (1 Kgs 11:12-13) and the promise of an abiding Davidic dynasty in

Jerusalem (1 Kgs 11:36; 15:4-5; 2 Kgs 8:19). David's devotion serves as a model for measuring the fidelity of subsequent kings (e.g., 1 Kgs 3:3; 11:4, 6, 38; 15:3, 11). The Lord's special favor to David is the basis of Jerusalem's divine protection when the Assyrian ruler Sennacherib attacks Hezekiah (2 Kgs 19:34; 20:5-6). When read against the backdrop of God's promise to David, the final paragraph of Kings (25:27-30) at least hints at a continued future for David's dynasty.

Prophetic Word

Prophets appear throughout Kings, interpreting events for the reader and signaling what to expect in the unfolding plot. Ahijah (1 Kgs 11:29-39; 14:7-16) prepares for the rise and fall of Jeroboam and for that of the entire Northern Kingdom. A mysterious "man of God from Judah" forecasts Josiah's reformation thirty-two chapters later (1 Kings 13). Elijah's threat in 1 Kings 21:21-24 helps shape the story of Ahab and his family. The assignment he passes on to Elisha (1 Kgs 19:15-17) prepares for events leading up to Jehu's revolution. One of the most bizarre stories in Kings is that of the prophet Micaiah (1 Kings 22). The Lord is so determined to accomplish the death of King Ahab that a lying spirit is commissioned to inspire a crowd of prophets with an unreliable prophetic message. The Lord's dependable provision of prophets to each generation means that neither Israel nor Judah could claim that their fate had taken them by surprise (2 Kgs 17:13, 33; 24:2).

Women

As is true of Joshua, Judges, and Samuel, Kings presents women as pivotal characters and actors in the unfolding of history. It sometimes casts women as villains (Solomon's wives, 1 Kgs 11:1-8; Jezebel, 18:19 and 21:5-15; Athaliah, 2 Kings 11). Bathsheba, in contrast, plays a vital role in the palace intrigue that leads to Solomon's accession (1 Kings 1). Two prostitutes and the Queen of Sheba enhance Solomon's reputation for wisdom (1 Kgs 3:16-28; 10:1-10). Women also play principal roles in certain prophetic narratives (1 Kgs 14:1-18; 17:8-24; 2 Kgs 4:1-37; 8:1-6). Finally, the prophet Huldah upholds the judgment of the book of the law on Judah, interprets the significance of Josiah's policies, and sets the course for the book's catastrophic finale (2 Kgs 22:14-20).

CHAPTER 9

THE BOOKS OF 1 AND 2 CHRONICLES

SHAPES AND STRUCTURES

C hronicles retells the history of Judah in the monarchy period from the perspective of the postexilic or Second Temple era. It is normally dated to about 400–350 BCE, in part because some of the genealogies at the beginning extend down that far in time (1 Chr 3:10-24; 9:3-34). Essentially the author has revised or rewritten Samuel and Kings in order to express certain theological opinions and to urge a postexilic audience to embrace these opinions and act upon them.

The story is tailored to the needs of readers living in Judah in the Second Temple period. Thus, the author used only those parts of Kings that deal with the kingdom of Judah, except when elements of the Northern Kingdom story were thoroughly intertwined with it. The negative material about David in 2 Samuel 9–20 was similarly excluded. This postexilic readership has come to the point where it esteems a written scripture, so there are frequent quotations or allusions to the Pentateuch and Psalms (for example, 1 Chronicles 16). Chronicles also uses the prophets Isaiah, Jeremiah, and Zechariah.

Chronicles falls into four principal divisions. It begins with genealogies (1 Chronicles 1–9). Then the stories of David's preparations for the temple (1 Chronicles 10–29) and Solomon's completion of it (2 Chronicles 1–9) are told. Finally, Chronicles recounts the reigns of the kings of Judah, centering on their policies concerning worship and the temple (2 Chronicles 10–36). Some basic theological focal points provide the groundwork for the way Chronicles retells history:

• the law of Moses (1 Chr 22:13; 2 Chr 33:8)
• God's promise to David (1 Chr 17:11-14)
• the Jerusalem Temple and its ritual (1 Chr 22:1; 28:19; 2 Chr 8:13)
• the "doctrine of retribution," which argues for a precise correspondence between one's behavior and one's destiny (2 Chr 20:20).

The author of Chronicles composed speeches and prayers for the main characters in order to present a particular theology and program of action to readers. Examples of these may be found in 1 Chronicles 22:5, 7-16; 28:2-10; 29:1-5, 10-19 (all by David); 2 Chronicles 13:4-12 (Abijah); and 30:6-9 (Josiah). Speeches by prophets repeatedly warn kings about impending judgments (e.g., 2 Chr 16:7-9).

In their speeches, these characters sometimes use scriptural texts to give authority to their statements. For example, 2 Chronicles 15:2-7 relies on Jeremiah 31:16 and Zephaniah 3:16; 2 Chronicles 16:7-9 quotes Zechariah 4:10; and 2 Chronicles 19:6-7 depends on Deuteronomy 10:17.

Two important structural techniques used in Chronicles are bracketing and pairing. An example of bracketing can be seen in the way David's involvement in the temple is "bookended" by his prayers in 1 Chronicles 17:16-27 and 29:10-19. In a similar way, speeches by Abijah (2 Chr 13:4-12) and Hezekiah (30:6-9) calling for repentance enclose the story of the divided kingdom.

The reader may explore the author's technique of pairing kings who play analogous roles by comparing David and Solomon.

The stories of David and Solomon are told in parallel ways to emphasize the similarities and close association between them. David prepares for what Solomon will do (1 Chronicles 22–26, 28–29), and Solomon does everything his father David planned for (2 Chronicles 2–7). Their interlocking accomplishments are further linked by David's speeches in 1 Chronicles 22:7-16; 28:2-10, 20-21; 29:1-5. In a similar way, the reforming kings Hezekiah and Josiah are minor versions of Solomon. Josiah's resemblance to Solomon is highlighted by the circumstance that each finds new roles for the Levites because they no longer needed to carry the ark (1 Chr 23:26-32; 2 Chr 35:3). Hezekiah and Josiah themselves are presented in parallel fashion as similar reformers of worship and Passover (2 Chr 29:3–31:21 and 34:3-13; 35:1-19).

ISSUES IN READING

One instructive way to read Chronicles is to compare it with the parallel text of Samuel and Kings.[1] Chronicles' changes and omissions uncover its author's special theology and opinions. One can easily see that the Chronicler has selected all positive items about David as temple builder and victor, but has left out negative items such as his adultery with Bathsheba and the rebellions of his sons. Sometimes the source material has been rearranged. For example, 1 Chronicles 11:10-47 (2 Sam 23:8-39) has been moved to an earlier point in David's career as an expression of the total popular support he enjoyed. Theological presuppositions led to the inclusion of some Levites to move the ark to Jerusalem in 1 Chronicles 15:26-27 (2 Sam 6:13-14) and the addition of the tent of meeting in 2 Chronicles 1:3-13 (1 Kgs 3:4-15). However, when making these comparisons, one needs to be aware that the Chronicler used a somewhat different text of Samuel-Kings from the one that has come down to us in the Hebrew Bible. This means that not all differences between Chronicles and Samuel-Kings represent actual authorial or editorial changes.

To us Chronicles sounds more like the work of a storyteller than a historian in the modern sense. For example, Chronicles enjoys recounting huge and exaggerated numbers for values (1 Chr 21:25; 22:14) or the size of armies (2 Chr 13:3, 17; 14:9). Otherwise unknown prophets are freely added to the ones already found in Samuel-Kings. Chronicles provides references to sources in the same way that Kings does, but these citations appear to be largely a matter of literary ornamentation and a literary strategy to increase the believability of what is being recounted. Whether the Chronicler actually had access to much in the way of trustworthy material apart from Samuel-Kings is a matter of scholarly dispute. At least the information given about Hezekiah's water tunnel (2 Chr 32:30) and Rehoboam's forts (2 Chr 11:5-10) appears to be reliable.

A number of scholars have concluded that 1 Chronicles 1–9 (genealogies) and 23–27 (temple personnel) represent later additions, though from a theological perspective similar to the rest of Chronicles. However, because these chapters show the same interest in David, Judah, and the concept of a unified Israel, they do not disturb the flow or harmony of the book in any way. Like the rest of the book, they reflect the so-called doctrine of retribution (5:1, 25-26; 10:13-14) and an interest in David's organization of temple personnel (6:31-48; 9:17-34).

THE PLOT OF CHRONICLES

Although Chronicles covers about the same history as Samuel and Kings, the approach to plot in Chronicles is significantly different. For one thing, the genealogical section reaches all the way back to Adam to initiate the story against a universal backdrop. Even more significant, Chronicles ends on a positive rather than negative note. Judah's destruction and exile is not the last word. Instead the plot concludes with permission for the exiles to return home. King Cyrus of Persia announces his intention to rebuild the temple at the command of "the God of heaven" (2 Chr 36:23). In contrast to Kings, which is an account of the kings and their rectitude or wrongdoing, Chronicles is really a history of the Jerusalem Temple and those who are devoted to it. While Kings looks back on the history of the nation to explain why it fell and went into exile, Chronicles looks forward in a positive way to the restored Jewish temple community of the Persian period.

Three Forces That Shape the Plot

Three factors work together to shape the plot of Chronicles. These are divine promise, the doctrine of retribution, and the temple. The individual events recounted in Chronicles coalesce into a plot because they are driven by God's explicit promises about David and the temple. This plot unfolds according to an inflexible rule of history, the so-called doctrine of retribution. Moreover, most episodes are focused on the Jerusalem Temple in some way. The short-term actions of the plot are performed by the kings, who behave virtuously or wickedly and reap the consequences of their acts. However, the larger plot trajectory centers on the temple, the Lord's house, which provides the backdrop and setting for the obedience or disobedience of the nation and its kings.

1. Divine Promise. The Lord's promises about the dynasty of David (1 Chr 17:11-14; 22:10; 28:4-7; 2 Chr 6:15-17; 7:17-18; 21:7) and the Jerusalem Temple (2 Chr 6:5-6; 12:13; 33:7) give motive power to the plot. They give the reader confident expectations about the ultimate future. David's special relationship with the Lord is set forth as early as 1 Chronicles 11:9; 14:2. The Lord unquestionably chose David, and his throne is to be established "forever" (1 Chr 22:10; 28:7; 2 Chr 6:10).[2] The Lord's special relationship with David is an unbreakable "covenant of salt" (2 Chr 13:5). Likewise, the Lord elected Solomon as David's heir (1 Chr 28:5-6). Jerusalem and its temple were also divinely chosen as the location for the Lord's name "forever." Yet the promise about David's descendants is qualified by the condition of royal obedience (1 Chr 28:8; 2 Chr 6:16; 7:17-18). In a similar way, the fate of the entire nation depends on the fidelity of the people (2 Chr 7:19-22, the "you" is plural; 33:8). The plot of Chronicles works itself out in the tension between unconditional promise and human transgression.

2. The Doctrine of Retribution. The plot of Chronicles also unfolds according to the formula of the doctrine of retribution. This cosmic game plan asserts that the unrighteous will suffer and the pious will be rewarded as a matter of course. David sets forth this principle in a positive fashion in his speech to Solomon: "Then you will prosper if you are careful to observe the statutes and the ordinances that the LORD commanded Moses for Israel" (1 Chr 22:13). Brief illustrations of this theology may be found in 2 Chronicles 25:20; 26:5; and 27:6. Thus Chronicles reports that obedient and reforming kings have numerous children, engage in impressive building projects (2 Chr 11:5-12; 26:9-10; 33:14), win victories (2 Chr 13:3-19; 14:9-15), and receive tribute. Disobedient kings are defeated, sicken with disease, and experience conspiracies. Rehoboam faces an invasion because of his apostasy from the law (2 Chr 12:1-5). Asa becomes diseased because of his alliance with a foreign power (2 Chr 16:7-10). Uzziah suffers from leprosy because of his objectionable attempt to offer incense (2 Chr 26:16-21).

Chronicles is less chronologically driven and linear than Kings is, in part because its plot is a repeated demonstration of the doctrine of retribution. Parallels and repetitive patterns in the careers of the kings repeatedly confirm this fundamental principle. The purpose is not so much to explain past disasters as to encourage present repentance. The prophet Azariah's words to Asa are also directed to the readers of Chronicles: "If you seek him, he will be found by you, but if you abandon him, he will abandon you" (2 Chr 15:2).

3. Temple. The Jerusalem Temple is the "stage set" against which much of the action of Chronicles is performed. It is already a feature of the introductory genealogy (1 Chr 6:10, 32) and plays a role of some sort in about two-thirds of the book's narrative chapters. Its location and plan are matters of divine revelation (1 Chr 21:18–22:1; 28:19; 2 Chr 3:1), confirmed twice by a descent of heavenly fire (1 Chr 21:26; 2 Chr 7:1). David prepares materials for the construction of the temple and organizes its staff (1 Chronicles 22–29). In 2 Chronicles 2–5, Solomon dutifully carries out all of David's plans (8:14-15) and dedicates the temple in chapters 6–7. Solomon, and later Jehoshaphat, expound the vital importance of the temple for national survival (6:20-40; 20:8-10).

Prayers made in the temple are heard in heaven (2 Chr 6:21; 7:14-15; 30:27). King Abijah insists that the chief transgression of the Northern Kingdom is its rejection of the true temple (13:4-12). The nation responds to the crisis of invasion under King Jehoshaphat by assembling in the temple at both the beginning and the end of the crisis (20:4-5, 27-28). Hezekiah likewise calls on northern Israelites to return to the temple (30:6-8). The reforms of Judah's virtuous kings involve temple restoration (Joash, 24:1-14; Hezekiah, 29:3-36; Josiah, 34:8-13). The crimes of Judah's last king Zedekiah "polluted the house of the LORD" (36:14). Chronicles describes in painful detail the destruction of the temple by the Babylonians and the plundering of its holy vessels (36:7, 10, 18-19). Finally, the last sentences of Chronicles conclude with the Lord's command to the Persian king Cyrus "to build him a house at Jerusalem."

Chronicles creates for the reader a world of ideological history. This is history as it ought to have been, a visionary history in which divine promise works itself out according to the rules of the doctrine of retribution in the context of the Jerusalem Temple. Genealogies (1 Chronicles 1–9) set the stage and connect readers to the saga that will unfold. These genealogies narrow the universal human story that begins with Adam down into the history of Israel, especially the tribes of the original readers (Judah, Levi, and Benjamin). Parts of these genealogies connect directly to the family trees of those who are reading the book (3:10-24; 9:3-34).

One way to understand the plot of Chronicles after the genealogies is to see it as a blending of a *linear plot* about the temple and a *cyclical plot* about the doctrine of retribution.

The Linear Temple Plot

Israel's story "as it ought to have been" means that all Israel immediately and overwhelmingly approves David as king with no conflict or dissension, and that he captures Jerusalem at once (1 Chronicles 11–12). The city is taken by "all Israel," and not just David's own troops (11:4). David's very first thought is to bring the ark there (chaps. 13–15). The king promptly establishes a procedure by which the priests continue the age-old sacrifice rituals at the tabernacle in Gibeon while the Levites take on new duties as ministers of the ark in Jerusalem (16). In this way, David himself establishes the service of thanksgiving and music in Jerusalem even before the temple itself can be constructed. In this transitional period, two parallel liturgies function simultaneously: sacrifice as commanded by Moses under the priests at Gibeon and worship by Levites at Jerusalem.

The capture of Jerusalem and the transfer of the ark there create in the reader an expectation that the temple is about to be built, but God's "no" to David in 1 Chronicles 17:4 throws up an obstacle. David cannot build because of his military career (as explained later in 22:8; 28:3). Yet God promises that David's son will construct the temple for David, giving rise to a suspenseful, dramatic tension that increases reader interest. David's wars (chaps. 18–20) are an uninterrupted, victorious progress illustrating the rewards of his perfect obedience. His single transgression is to take a census, but he quickly repents of this (21). The plot pressure builds as David selects the site for the future temple in accordance with the clear designation of the Lord (21:18–22:1). He makes detailed preparations for Solomon to build the temple after his death, gathering materials and organizing workers, Levites, and priests (chaps. 22–26). The Levites had carried the ark under Moses (15:15), but now the ark's permanent location in Jerusalem means that David can assign them a new set of duties (23:25-32), organizing them in a detailed way (chaps. 23, 25–26). David also makes organizational arrangements for the priests based on the Lord's guidance expressed by the casting of lots (24:1-19; see also 28:13; 2 Chr 8:14; 23:18).

The reader's encounter with ideological history continues when Solomon is acclaimed as king entirely without conflict (1 Chr 23:1; 29:22-25). God has chosen him (28:10; 29:1) as a man of peace (22:8-10). David instructs him to build the temple (22:7-16; 28:2-10, 20-21). To encourage enthusiasm and build reader interest, David utters dramatic imperatives: "Now begin the work" (22:16), "go and build" (v. 19), "be strong, and act" (28:10), "be strong and of good courage, and act" (v. 20).

After this prolonged buildup, Solomon finally constructs the temple according to David's plans and dedicates it (2 Chronicles 2–7). In so doing, Solomon merges the priestly sacrifice at Gibeon with the worship of the Levites at Jerusalem, both of which had previously been organized by David. At the temple dedication, fire falls from heaven and God's glory fills the building (7:1-2). The drawn-out plot tension is finally relaxed as the text repeatedly asserts that Solomon "finished" (5:1; 7:11; 8:16; cf. David's command in 1 Chr 28:20). The temple is a most wonderful institution. It is the focus of the Lord's promise to be eternally connected to Israel (2 Chr 2:4-5; 7:12-16).

At this point, the plot reaches its high point in a golden age of Israel's relationship with the Lord. However, this good news of God's promises about temple and dynasty (2 Chr 7:17-18) exists in profound tension with the corresponding divine threat of national destruction voiced in 7:19-22. For now, though, Solomon is the perfect king, engaging in no idolatry and enjoying God's blessing (chaps. 8–9). For example, King Huram of Tyre gives *him* cities (8:2), the exact reverse of what 1 Kings 9:11 reports! Solomon carefully conforms to all of David's earlier worship arrangements (8:12-15).

The threat of 2 Chronicles 7:19-22 begins to unfold when the Northern Kingdom repudiates David and the temple, and both kingdoms practice widespread disobedience. Although there are ups and downs, the plot now trends downward from the high point of Solomonic glory to crash finally into defeat and exile. One current of disobedience centers on the Northern Kingdom's repudiation of David and the Jerusalem Temple (10:19), although at various times loyal northerners continue to support the Davidic throne and the temple (11:13-16; 15:9). King Abijah's speech to northern Israelites underscores the enormity of their rejection of the legitimate priesthood and correct worship (13:4-12). He lists six items that prove Judah's religious loyalty: Aaronic priests, Levites, morning and evening sacrifices, incense, showbread, and temple lamps (vv. 10-11). Subsequent holy war victory proves him right.

However, Judah too engages in rebellion against the Lord. Its kings make treaties with foreign powers (2 Chr 16:7-9; 28:16), associate with the wicked kings of Israel (20:35-37; 22:3-5), encourage worship outside Jerusalem (21:11-15; 28:24-25), and commit pagan idolatry (24:18-19; 25:14; 28:2-4, 23; 33:2-7). Nevertheless, there are also great reforming kings who undo these offenses and restore justice and proper worship. The important reformers are Asa (14:3-5; 15:8-18), Jehoshaphat (17:7-9; 19:4-11), Hezekiah (chaps. 29–31), and Josiah (chap. 34; 35:1-19). Both Hezekiah and Josiah, for example, reorganize temple operations according to the model of David and Solomon (31:2-19; 35:2-5). Indeed Josiah's Passover actually surpasses any ever celebrated in the monarchy period (35:18). In spite of these reforms, however, Huldah's prophecy makes it clear that the die is cast and that God will destroy Jerusalem (34:24-25).

In the concluding chapter, Judah's fortunes crash. The last four kings are all wicked. Jehoahaz is exiled to Egypt and Jehoiakim and Jehoiachin are exiled to Babylon. Zedekiah and his leadership sink so low that they "pollute" the temple (2 Chr 36:14). Out of compassion for the people and the temple, the Lord has sent many prophets with warning messages over time, but these

157

prophets have been ignored (vv. 15-16) and, in the case of Zechariah (24:20-22), even killed.

Defeat and exile are followed by a desolate pause of seventy years (2 Chr 36:21, a figure based not on actual history but on Jer 25:11-12; 29:10). Although punishment had to follow such appalling crimes, this is not the end. In the long term, the Lord can be expected to remain true to the covenant with Israel (1 Chr 16:15-17; 2 Chr 6:14) and true to the "forever" promises made about the temple (2 Chr 2:4; 7:12-16). Consequently, the last sentences of Chronicles move the story forward to the first year of Cyrus and the Lord's command for him "to build him a house at Jerusalem" (36:23). The book ends with a stirring injunction from Cyrus to those who wish to return to be the community of this reconstructed temple: "Let him go up!" In other words, the culmination and fulfillment of the plot of Chronicles turns out to be the postexilic temple community, none other than the original readership. Ultimately, Chronicles is not just about the past, but about its own Second Temple–period readers as well.

The Cyclical Plot of Retribution

Embedded in the linear plot about promise and punishment centered on the temple is a cyclical plot that repeatedly demonstrates the doctrine of retribution. Together the kings from Rehoboam to Josiah form a cumulative presentation of evidence that one's fate depends directly on one's behavior before God. Some kings are viewed in a wholly negative light and suffer corresponding punishments (Jehoram, Joash, Ahaz, and Amon). A couple of others are fully obedient and are rewarded (Abijah, Jotham).

Most, however, have a mixed history, even the great reforming kings. Rehoboam provides the paradigm. First he is obedient and is rewarded (2 Chronicles 11). Then he disobeys and is punished (12:1-4). Finally he repents and is once more rewarded (vv. 5-12). More common is a two-step pattern in which a period of obedience and reward is followed by a phase of disobedience and associated penalty. This holds true for Asa, Joash, Amaziah, and Uzziah. For the reforming kings Jehoshaphat and Hezekiah, the period of disobedience is only a brief one at the end of their reigns (20:35-37; 32:25). In the case of Josiah, his act of disobedience is introduced by the author in a clumsy way and leads immediately to his premature death (35:20-24). Somewhat ironi-cally, given his villainous role in Kings, it is only Manasseh whose career starts with wrongdoing (33:1-11) and then moves to repen-tance and a final episode of good behavior (vv. 12-16). The life histories of these various kings serve to confirm the principle of retribution and warn readers to avoid sin and practice virtue.

The value of sincere repentance is a corollary of the axiom of retribution. Rehoboam, Manasseh, and to a lesser extent Hezekiah, illustrate the principle that "humbling" oneself before God in repentance can lead to forgiveness and well-being (2 Chr 12:6-7; 32:26; 33:12-13). To quote David: "If you seek him, he will be found by you; but if you forsake him, he will abandon you for-ever" (1 Chr 28:9). Other speeches also express this call for repentance (2 Chr 7:14; 15:2; 30:9).

Battle accounts provide Chronicles with an opportunity to show off the doctrine of retribution in the careers of good kings. Their reliance on God or exemplary repentance results in stu-pendous victories obtained as a reward. The impact of these vic-tories on the reader is magnified by the use of huge numbers for the rival armies (for example, Asa versus the Ethiopians, 2 Chr 14:9). Great victories are won by Abijah (13:13-19), Asa (14:9-15), Jehoshaphat (20:22-25), and Amaziah (25:11-12).

CONTEXTS AND AUDIENCES

For the original audience, reading Chronicles would have meant experiencing something like a time warp. The past and present are brought together onto the same screen, so that Chronicles presents the ancient past to its readers in a familiar and contemporary way. Worshipers in the early monarchy period engage in ceremonial patterns and arrangements completely familiar to postexilic readers. Contemporary liturgical practices are traced back to David and Solomon (e.g., 2 Chr 5:11-13). The psalms sung now were also sung then (1 Chr 16:7-36). The cur-rent separation of the priests into two families, their organization into twenty-four groups, and even minor details about the guilds and tasks of the Levites, have remained unchanged since the reign of David (1 Chronicles 23–26).

The primary intended audience of Chronicles was the Jewish community in and around Jerusalem in the Second Temple period. They were subjects of the Persian Empire, but looked back to a strong tradition of national and religious independence. Life was not unbearable under Persian domination, but their political subjugation still rankled. Thus Ezra 9:8-9 and Nehemiah 9:37 speak of their situation as virtual slavery. The fictional book of Esther provides a narrative window on the potential insecurity of life under the Persians, for the empire was dangerously unstable at times. This small community faced the multiple challenges of hostile neighbors, demoralizing nostalgia (Ezra 3:12), poverty (Neh 5:2-5), underpopulation (Neh 7:4), faithless religious behavior (Isa 57:3-13; 65:3-7, 11; 66:17), and the danger of losing its identity through intermarriage (Ezra 9:1-2; 10:18-44). The discontinuity of exile and the claims of other groups to be the true heirs of preexilic Israel called into question their legitimacy as God's people (Ezra 4:1-2).

To this audience, Chronicles speaks a strong message of encouragement and identity. The initial genealogies link them directly to their identity as God's chosen people. Chronicles underscores the divine election of David, Solomon, Jerusalem, the priests and Levites, and especially the temple (1 Chr 15:2; 28:4; 29:1; 2 Chr 6:5-6; 12:13; 29:11; 33:7). It does not matter that they have no king now, for in fact the throne and kingdom properly belong to the Lord (1 Chr 17:14; 28:5; 29:11, 23; 2 Chr 13:8). Their devotion to the written law is a sign of their connection with the authentic people of God (2 Chr 31:4; 34:29-32). King Abijah's address to the Northern Kingdom army speaks directly to readers' genuine identity as God's true people. They still hold to all six of the identifying marks of loyalty to which Abijah pointed: Aaronic priests, Levites, morning and evening sacrifices, incense, showbread, and temple lamps (2 Chr 13:8-12).

Probably some factions objected that the reconstructed temple was not the legitimate house of the Lord. After all, pagan Persian authorities had authorized and financed it (2 Chr 36:23; Ezra 1:4; 3:7; 6:3-5, 9-10). To meet such objections, Chronicles seeks to convince readers that the present temple truly is God's house. Its site was chosen and revealed by the Lord. The authority of God's revelation to Moses and David lies behind even minor details of its arrangements (1 Chr 28:19; 2 Chr 8:13-15; 30:16).

There was another controversy over whether the city of Jerusalem, the land, and its people had become permanently unclean because of exile and alien occupation. Was Jerusalem permanently polluted because of the blood shed in it when captured (Lam 4:4-5; Ezek 9:7)? Could the produce of an unclean land be brought for sacrifice (the point of Haggai's question in Hag 2:13-14)? Could priests born in exile in an unclean land perform effective sacrifices (the question lying behind Zech 3:1-5)? God's answer to Hezekiah's prayer in 2 Chronicles 30:18-20 seeks to resolve this issue. Sincerity of heart is more important than ritual cleanliness.

The temple vessels play a significant role in connecting the temple of the past to the temple of the readers' own day. Chronicles often mentions these vessels as the first temple is prepared for (1 Chr 18:8; 22:19; 28:13-18), completed (2 Chr 4:11, 16; 5:1, 5), and reformed (24:14). Then in describing the fall of Judah, Chronicles repeatedly alludes to their loss to the Babylonians (36:7, 10, 18). According to Ezra 1:7-11; 5:14-15, the returning exiles brought some of these vessels back from Babylon for use in the newly rebuilt temple. Consequently, the postexilic readers of Chronicles would feel a sense of connection with the past when they read about them. At the same time, this emphasis on temple vessels helps to legitimate the Second Temple.

However, Chronicles also appears to be addressed in a roundabout way to a second audience. The adherents of Yahweh in the north part of the land (Samaria) did not worship at the temple or acknowledge the legitimacy and religious authority of the Jerusalem community. To this group, Chronicles emphasizes that true Israel is a single people and that, in the past, devout northerners had also been part of the temple community. Northerners make up a considerable component in those who support David's kingship (1 Chronicles 12). "All Israel" makes David king (11:1) and captures Jerusalem (v. 4). "All Israel" brings the ark to Jerusalem (13:5-6; 15:3) and helps dedicate the temple (2 Chr 7:6, 8). The people of Samaria dutifully obey the prophet Oded in 2 Chronicles 28:8-15. There are even northern tribes living in Jerusalem at the time of the return from exile (1 Chr 9:3).

To these descendants of the former Northern Kingdom, Chronicles is a call to revere the Jerusalem Temple as legitimate. History is said to provide examples for them to imitate. Immediately after the division of the kingdom, loyal northerners come back to worship in Jerusalem (2 Chr 11:13-17). Others join King Asa in worship and agree together to seek the Lord (15:9-

15). Hezekiah invites northerners to come back to the temple for Passover, although only a few respond (2 Chr 30:1-11), and special arrangements are made for them (vv. 17-19). A similar thing happens in the reign of Josiah (34:33; 35:17-18). This secondary audience of northern outsiders is intended to overhear King Abijah's condemnation of their ancestors (13:4-12). They are challenged to repent and rejoin their kinfolk in proper worship at the Jerusalem Temple.

Chronicles calls on readers from any era who read it as canonic scripture to be faithful to God and to repent of past infidelity. David, Solomon, and the great reforming kings serve as models of faithful obedience. The good news implicit in the doctrine of retribution is that God is gracious (2 Chr 36:15-16) and that heartfelt repentance is able to call down mercy (20:20). As God proclaims to Solomon, "If my people who are called by my name humble themselves, pray, seek my face, and turn from their wicked ways, then I will hear from heaven, and will forgive their sin and heal their land" (7:14). Penitent kings like Rehoboam and Manasseh (12:12; 33:12-13) provide readers with examples to imitate.

This call for a change of heart is reinforced by the prophetic warnings that the author adds to the story at every turn. Asa's quick response to the admonition of the prophet Azariah provides a prime example of what readers ought to do (2 Chr 15:1-15). Jehoshaphat is addressing the reader directly when he declares, "Believe in the LORD your God and you will be established; believe his prophets" (20:20). Fidelity in the practice of worship is a vital component of proper repentance (29:5-11), and this has been demonstrated by Hezekiah and Josiah (chaps. 29–31, 34–35). In this way, readers are encouraged to manifest their repentance by worshiping at the temple and by bringing generous offerings to it, just as their ancestors did (1 Chr 29:8-9; 2 Chr 31:4-10).

THEMES

Worship

Chronicles emphasizes that the high point of community life is joyful worship in song, prayer, and praise. The ark is moved with jubilation (1 Chr 15:16, 28), and joyful national celebrations mark the other important turning points of Israel's history (1 Chr 12:38-40; 29:17; 2 Chr 7:10; 20:27; 30:26). Psalm 106:1 is used repeatedly as a joyful refrain (1 Chr 16:34, 41; 2 Chr 5:13; 7:3, 6; 20:21). Joy is more important than liturgical fine points, which can be modified if need be (2 Chr 7:7-10; 29:34; 30:2-4). Prayer and good intentions can cover any technical problems (30:18-20). Even warfare is treated as a liturgical activity (20:18-22).

Temple Holiness

Chronicles is careful to defend the spatial holiness of the temple. Thus, although the Levites usually carry the ark, they have to turn it over to priests, who take it into the most holy part of the temple (2 Chr 5:4-5, 7). Chronicles reports that Solomon moved his Egyptian wife out of range of the temple's holiness (8:11). Princess Jehoshabeath (foster mother to baby King Joash) is turned into a wife of the high priest in order to sanction her residence in the temple (22:11). In the coup against Athaliah, non-priests are carefully kept out of the temple by converting the guards described in Kings into priests and Levites (23:4, 6; contrast 2 Kgs 11:5-7). Doorkeepers are stationed to keep out ritually unclean persons (v. 19). King Uzziah attempts to trespass on the domain of the holy by entering the temple to burn incense, which only priests could do. Even though the faithful priests try to block his royal insolence, Uzziah is quickly struck by unclean leprosy and has to be hurried out of the holy space of the temple (26:16-20).

Levites

Chronicles is intensely concerned with the rights and duties of the Levites, who owe their position to David (1 Chr 9:22; 2 Chr 8:14). Levites are praised for their fidelity (2 Chr 11:14; 29:34), although they are not completely exempt from criticism (2 Chr 24:5-6). Their genealogies and duties receive careful attention in 1 Chronicles 6 and 23–26. They are divided into families that have specific tasks (1 Chr 15:16-22). Primarily they are singers who lead the people in praise (1 Chr 15:16-22; 16:4-5, 37-42; 2 Chr 5:12-13; 8:14; 20:19; 29:25-30; 35:15). They also serve as doorkeepers who guard the holiness of the temple (2 Chr 23:19) and as liturgical assistants (1 Chr 9:28-32; 23:32). They prepare the showbread and grain offerings (1 Chr 23:28-29) and under emergency conditions perform other quasi-priestly tasks (2 Chr 29:34; 35:11). The transport of the ark is their prerogative (1 Chr 15:2; 2 Chr 5:4-5). Thus David's first attempt to move the ark led to disaster, but the proper use of Levites ensured success on the second try (1 Chr 15:2, 13-15). Levites also serve as teachers (2 Chr 17:7-9; 35:3), judges (2 Chr 19:8-11), scribes (1 Chr 24:6; 2 Chr 34:13), and prophets (1 Chr 25:5; 2 Chr 20:14-17).

Priests and Prophets

Chronicles insists on a clear distinction between the respective roles of priests and Levites and traces this differentiation back to the arrangements of Moses and David (1 Chr 6:31-32, 48-49). It was David who put the Levites in charge of song and service, but the special privileges of the priests are even more ancient and go back to Moses and Aaron (1 Chr 23:13; 24:19). The proper role of priests is to make sacrifice for atonement (1 Chr 6:49) and to perform other special tasks centered on sacrificial ritual (2 Chr 23:18; 30:16).[3]

Chronicles describes an unbroken string of prophets who function as mediators between the Lord and the people. They warn the kings and people, but also serve as intercessors. Familiar prophets appear, such as Isaiah (2 Chr 32:20) and Jeremiah (35:25), along with otherwise unknown ones like Azariah (15:1) and Oded (28:9). Chronicles also identifies certain Levites and temple singers as prophets (1 Chr 25:1-5; 2 Chr 20:14). Prophets are also seen as authors, and their works supposedly served as historical sources for Chronicles: Samuel, Nathan, and Gad (1 Chr 29:29), Nathan and Ahijah (2 Chr 9:29), Shemaiah and Iddo (12:15), Isaiah (26:22; 32:32), and so forth.

CHAPTER 10

THE BOOKS OF EZRA AND NEHEMIAH

SHAPES AND STRUCTURES

E zra and Nehemiah make up a single book in the Jewish canonical tradition, although Christians have separated them since the third century. Because the story of Ezra's reform is not complete until Nehemiah 8, it is best to read Ezra and Nehemiah together.

Ezra-Nehemiah is a complex book. In part, this may be because of a history of composition that involved several stages. However, its complexity also reflects the use of numerous sources. Two primary sources have been identified. The first of these is an account of Ezra's mission. This is a mixture of first-person and third-person reports about the success of Ezra's official assignment to bring God's law to the returned Jews. This source provided the foundation for Ezra 7–10 and Nehemiah 8–9. The other primary source is the "words of Nehemiah" (Neh 1:1), usually labeled the "Memoirs of Nehemiah." This is a first-person account and justification of Nehemiah's public career, conventionally addressed to God. This source lies behind Nehemiah 1–7; 11:1-2; 12:31-43; 13:4-31. It concludes, "Remember me, O my God, for good" (that is, "to my credit"). Most scholars consider this an authentic autobiography. Other lesser sources are present as well. Some of these were included in the larger source documents.

- copies or imitations of official documents: Ezra 1:2-4; 6:3-5
- letters: Ezra 4:8-22; 5:7-17; 6:6-12; 7:12-26; Neh 6:2-9
- inventory lists: Ezra 1:9-11; 8:26-27
- rosters and census rolls: Ezra 2:1-70 (= Neh 7:7-72a); 8:1-14; 10:18-43; Neh 3:1-32; 9:38–10:27; 11:3-24, 25-36; 12:1-26.

Another curious feature of Ezra-Nehemiah, created in part by this lavish employment of sources, is an alternation between the Hebrew language, in which most of the book is written, and Aramaic, the language of the Persian government. Ezra 4:8–6:18 and 7:12-26 are in Aramaic.

Ezra-Nehemiah depicts the struggles of the first generations of returned Jewish exiles to revive their religious and community life as part of the Persian Empire. In the face of prodigious difficulties, these returnees were able to achieve three crucial accomplishments.

- Led by Sheshbazzar and Zerubbabel, they rebuilt the Jerusalem temple (Ezra 1–6).
- Through the efforts of Ezra, they purified their community through fidelity to God's law (Ezra 7–10; Nehemiah 8–10).
- Under the leadership of Nehemiah, they reconstructed the wall of Jerusalem (Nehemiah 1–7, 11–13).

The correlation of these three successive national achievements provides Ezra-Nehemiah with its basic structure: rebuilding the temple, reforming the community, and reconstructing the city wall. These three subplots culminate in the shared climax of a renewal of the covenant (Nehemiah 8–10). The first and last of these accomplishments are summarized by parallel formulas in the work's two languages: "This house was finished" (Ezra 6:15, Aramaic); "the wall was finished" (Neh 6:15, Hebrew).

The increasingly personal character of the presentation also serves as a significant structuring device. The focus moves from collective history (Ezra 1–6) to the story of Ezra told in both auto-biographical and third-person fashion (Ezra 7–10; Nehemiah 8–10), to the career of Nehemiah recounted in a predominantly autobiographical mode (Nehemiah 1–7, 11–13).

Less visible structuring devices are also at work. Turning points in the narrative are marked by linking statements: "after this" (Ezra 7:1), "after these things" (Ezra 9:1), and "before this" (Neh 13:4). Brief summary statements hold together narrative units. For example, Ezra 4:4-5 concludes and integrates the report of initial work on the temple found in 3:2–4:3. Ezra 6:13-15 performs the same function in regard to the resumption of temple work in 5:1–6:12. The technique of contrasting dialogue is used to advance the narrative in Nehemiah 4:10-14 and 5:1-5.[1] Another structuring technique is provided by regular references to dates. The writer dates nearly all significant events. These include the start of sacrifice at the restored altar (Ezra 3:6), the completion of the temple and the first Passover there (6:15, 19), finishing the city wall (Neh 6:15), reading the law (8:2), and the penitential national assembly (9:1).

ISSUES IN READING

Ezra-Nehemiah works better as a piece of literature than as a book of historiography. Although most of its sources are considered to be reliable, the overall presentation of events contains significant distortions. For example, there is a chronological gap of more than fifty years between the completion of the temple at the end of Ezra 6 and the start of Ezra's mission in chapter 7. Because the work's theological goals are more important than its historiographic purposes, the text just collapses this half-century with a simple "after this" (7:1).

Another example of the work's molding of history to suit its own purposes is the unexplained replacement of Sheshbazzar by the more significant figure of Zerubbabel. Although Sheshbazzar was the original guardian of the temple vessels and initiator of temple construction (Ezra 1:7-11; 5:14-16), he simply disappears. Zerubbabel abruptly appears in his place in connection with temple construction (Ezra 3:2; 5:2). As a descendant of David's royal family, Zerubbabel may have been more compatible with the author's desire to proclaim the legitimacy of the new temple.

A third instance of historical impreciseness involves the use of an Aramaic language source in Ezra 4:6-24 that describes an exchange of letters involving a Persian king. Although this is cited as an obstruction of the goal of finishing the temple in the reign of King Darius, these letters self-evidently refer instead to the much later controversy over rebuilding the wall of Jerusalem (vv. 12-13). They plainly involve King Artaxerxes, who did not come to the throne until fifty years after the temple was finished.[2] Presumably the author included this material at a historically inopportune place in order to make a literary and theological point about the general sort of opposition faced by all those who sought to restore aspects of the postexilic community. Again, the requirements of literary structure and theology take precedence over historical precision.

A more flagrant example of literary sleight of hand involves the overlapping of the careers of Ezra and Nehemiah that takes place in Nehemiah 8 (and 12:26, 36). The date of Ezra's commission was apparently 458 BCE (year seven of Artaxerxes) and that of Nehemiah's appointment definitely 445 BCE (year twenty of Artaxerxes).[3] An overlap between the two would only be possible if Ezra's mission lasted thirteen years or more and the events of Nehemiah 8 and 9 took place near the beginning of Nehemiah's appointment. However, it is very improbable that Ezra would have waited until thirteen years into his mission to read the law to the people.

Ezra and Nehemiah are actually directly associated together only in Nehemiah 8:9 (and less directly so in 12:26, 36). There are good reasons to think that Nehemiah's name has been subsequently inserted into 8:9 (for example, the main verb is singular, not plural). A careful examination of the source material about Ezra suggests that the events surrounding Ezra's act of reading the law (in Nehemiah 8–9 and perhaps 10) actually took place immediately following the events reported in Ezra 7–8. In other words, Ezra's mission reached its climax in less than a year and concluded over a decade *before* Nehemiah appeared on the scene.[4] The author's coordination of Ezra and Nehemiah may have been bad history, but it made for coherent theological literature. The inspiring climactic scene of reading the law of God and the people's wholehearted reception of it (Nehemiah 8–10) is no longer simply the last act of Ezra's mission. Now it has become the high point that climaxes the parallel restoration projects of both famous leaders.

THE PLOT OF EZRA-NEHEMIAH

The plot of Ezra-Nehemiah describes three reform actions, each initiated by a Persian king. King Cyrus decrees the return of the exiles and the rebuilding of the temple (Ezra 1–6). Next King Artaxerxes commissions Ezra to restore the law of God to the community, leading to the dissolution of mixed marriages (Ezra 7–10). Later this same Artaxerxes appoints Nehemiah as governor in order to rebuild Jerusalem and its defensive wall (Nehemiah 1–7). These three reforms come together and reach a resounding climax with the reading of God's law before a national assembly and the community's promise to obey it (Nehemiah 8–10). A few loose ends remain to be tied up, and Nehemiah does so with a series of societal reforms (Nehemiah 11–13).

The driving force of the plot is the anticipated achievement of the three goals of restoration encouraged by the Persian kings. These three subplots move in corresponding patterns.

• God inspires the king to commission a reform (Ezra 1:1-4; 7:6, 27; Neh 1:11; 2:8).
• The reform leaders are equipped with what they need to attain their goal (money and temple vessels: Ezra 1:6-11; 8:24-30; letters of authorization: Ezra 7:11-26; Neh 2:7-9).
• Central characters lead exiles back (Ezra 1:11 and 2:2; 7:7-8; 8:15-32).
• Resistance and obstacles to the anticipated goal develop (neighboring peoples: Ezra 3:3; 4:1-6; mixed marriages: Ezra 9:1-4, 10-15; Sanballat and Tobias: Neh 2:10, 19; 4:1-3, 7-8; 6:1-14, 17-19).
• Leaders engage in decisive action and achieve the reforming goal (Ezra 6:22; 10:44; Neh 6:15-16).

Rebuilding the Temple (Ezra 1–6)

The word of God through Jeremiah (see Jer 29:10) and the Lord's action on the psyche of Cyrus initiate an effort to restore both the temple and the community that will worship there (Ezra

1:1-4). The return of the original temple vessels legitimates the rebuilt temple (vv. 7-11). The inclusion of a list of returnees gives the reader an impression of a comprehensive group (chap. 2). No problems arise in rebuilding the altar, initiating proper sacrifices on it, gathering materials, and starting the foundational work (chap. 3). Tension is first introduced into the plot by apprehension about neighboring peoples (3:3) and the mixed reaction that greets the temple foundation (vv. 12-13).[5]

The initial anxiety becomes concrete in the obstacles set up in Ezra 4. This exchange of letters illustrates the sort of opposition that freezes construction for years (vv. 4-5, 24). Eventually it requires the cooperation of the prophets, the high priest, and the Davidic descendant Zerubbabel to restart the process (5:1-2). Tattenai's opposition is overcome with God's help (v. 5), the politically astute wording of the Jewish reply (vv. 11-17), and the reconfirmation of Cyrus's decree by King Darius (6:1-12). The reader is delighted by the irony that Tattenai, as governor of Beyond the River, must now financially support the project he had opposed (vv. 8-9)! The goal of the first plot trajectory is reached by the paired "command of the God of Israel" and "decree of Cyrus" (v. 14). The achievement of the objective of the plot is signaled by joy, offerings, and Passover (vv. 16-22). A reference to God's effect over the king's heart (v. 22) returns in a satisfying circle to the decree of Cyrus that first launched this subplot (1:1).

Reforming the Community (Ezra 7–10)

Once again the story line is set in motion by the Persian king, prompted by God (Ezra 7:6, 27-28). The reader is persuaded to trust Ezra as a man of excellent pedigree (vv. 1-5) and personal dedication (v. 10). An apparently official document and use of eyewitness language (v. 28) enhance the credibility of the narrative. Ezra's mission is to investigate matters with regard to the law (v. 14), give financial support to the temple liturgy (vv. 15-20), and teach and enforce God's law (vv. 25-26). Attainment of Ezra's goals seems in reach as he leads back an impressive group of exiles (8:1-14), appropriately recruits Levites (vv. 15-20), enjoys divine protection (v. 31), and makes proper delivery of the temple vessels (vv. 24-30, 33-34). He carries out his task of arranging support for the temple services (v. 36).

Then an ugly obstacle to further success arises in the form of mixed marriages (Ezra 9:1-2). Ezra's extreme reactions provide a literary signal of the gravity of this transgression (vv. 3-4). His confessional prayer is a first step in achieving a resolution of this problem. It also serves to remind the reader of the obstacles that lie in the way of achieving a purified community (vv. 7, 10-12, 14), but also of the gracious purposes of God (vv. 8-9, 13, 15). A spontaneous national assembly and a "grass roots" plan of action overcome the obstacle of intermarriage (10:1-4). The public is so fervent in their commitment that they seek to excommunicate the offenders and dedicate their property to God (v. 8). The text seeks to convince the reader that the appointment of a task force is a good and sensible plan (vv. 13-14). The successful conclusion of this investigative commission's work (v. 16) is underscored by the inclusion of a long list of cases (vv. 18-43). Realization of the goal of the subplot is indicated by the sweeping divorce apparently reported in verse 44.[6]

Rebuilding the City Wall (Nehemiah 1–7)

The third subplot again begins with a Persian king. The primary narrative problem of Jerusalem's insecurity is introduced in Nehemiah 1:3. First, however, an initial subproblem of gaining a favorable hearing from "this man," that is, the king (v. 11), must be resolved. By prayer (1:5-11; 2:4) and skillful speech (2:3, 5) Nehemiah overcomes this first obstacle.

However, other obstacles quickly arise, especially in the form of Nehemiah's archenemies, Sanballat and Tobiah (Neh 2:10). Nehemiah makes his inspection of the demolished walls while keeping his mission a secret (vv. 11-16). When he finally reveals his secret mission, it is greeted with enthusiasm (vv. 17-18), but also by renewed external opposition (v. 19). As the plot unfolds, the barriers to success are many: mockery (4:1-3), threats of attack (vv. 7-8, 11-12), and the difficulty of the task (v. 10). The geography of 4:7 indicates to the reader that the threats come from all four points of the compass at once: Sanballat on the north in Samaria, Tobiah the Ammonite on the east, Arabs on the south, and the city of Ashdod on the west. Nonetheless, Nehemiah meets each challenge with prayer (vv. 4-5, 9), wise strategies (vv. 9, 13, 16-18, 21-23), and encouraging speech (vv. 14, 19-20). In chapter 5, a new obstacle to completing the wall is revealed. Internal social oppression is causing discord (5:1-5). Again, Nehemiah deftly handles the problem (vv. 6-13). His personal defense before God continues to build up his character in the eyes of the reader (vv. 14-19).

Impediments to success reach their peak in chapter 6. Nehemiah's enemies repeatedly scheme against him, advancing from devious invitations (vv. 1-2) through open accusations of treason (vv. 6-7) to an attempt to destroy his reputation (vv. 10-11). Even prophets treacherously oppose him (vv. 12-14). Nevertheless, he cleverly deals with them all and through God's help finally achieves the goal of this third subplot (vv. 15-16). However, the wall is not yet dedicated, so that the story of Nehemiah remains open-ended until after the decisive climax of the book. In fact, Nehemiah is confronted with yet another new problem in the shape of Jerusalem's low population (7:4). He begins to address this predicament by consulting the same roster of returnees that was employed at the start of the first plot movement (Ezra 2:1-70 = Neh 7:6-73) in order to prepare for an assembly (v. 5). However the climax must come first, before this fresh plot line can be resolved.

Climax: Hearing and Doing the Law (Nehemiah 8–10)

Ezra's act of reading the law to the assembly of Israel and the resulting national confession and covenant serve as the climax for all three subplots. The three story lines about restoration and reformation are woven together into a single overarching plot movement by these events. The joyous celebration of the Feast of Booths that follows Ezra's reading of the law book (Neh 8:13-18) links back to the celebrations that greeted the completion of the altar and temple (Ezra 3:4-5, 10-13; 6:16-22). It also points forward to the upcoming dedication of the city wall (Neh 12:27-43). The nation's confessional prayer (Neh 9:6-37) connects to that of Ezra in the second plot movement (Ezra 9:6-15).[7]

The previously separate characters of Ezra and Nehemiah now appear together. Nehemiah shares in Ezra's task of teaching the law (Neh 8:9), just as Ezra will eventually take part in the dedication of the city wall Nehemiah has built (12:36). Everything works together to create a positive and upbeat finale. All hear the law and are attentive (8:1-3). All are helped to understand (vv. 7-8, 12). Hearing the law makes people eager to study it (v. 13). This in turn leads to a celebration of a Feast of Booths that is perfect in every way (vv. 14-18) and then to a ceremony of genuine national repentance (9:1-37).

The final step in the climax is a formal covenant to keep the law (9:38) agreed to by an impressive list of notables (including Nehemiah, 10:1). The content of the nation's mutual agreements involves mixed marriages, keeping the sabbath and the sabbath year, arrangements for the support of the temple and its staff, and offering first fruits and the firstborn (vv. 30-39). These various agreements provide a catalog of unfinished business for Nehemiah to deal with as the book draws to a close.

Denouement: Further Reforms by Nehemiah (Nehemiah 11–13)

In a conventional plot, a final section of denouement ties up loose ends and answers questions. Following the rousing climax of Ezra's reading of the law, the concluding reforms of Nehemiah serve as a denouement for Ezra-Nehemiah as a whole. Remaining situations and problems are resolved. Nehemiah adroitly solves the predicament of Jerusalem's low population (Nehemiah 11), then dedicates the city wall in a joyous celebration (12:27-43). Note how verse 43 parallels Ezra 3:13.

"On that day" (Neh 12:44) temple staff and support are properly arranged. "On that day" (13:1), "Israel" disengages itself from outsiders (13:3). In fact, even "before this," Nehemiah has evicted his nemesis Tobiah from a temple chamber and reinstated the legitimate temple vessels there (13:4-9). A final burst of reforms quickly deals with various questions left open by the covenant agreement of 10:28-39. Nehemiah deals in turn with support for the Levites (vv. 10-13; cf. 10:38-39), violations of the sabbath (vv. 15-22; 10:31), mixed marriages (vv. 23-29; 10:30), and provision for offerings of firewood and first fruits (v. 31; 10:34, 35-37).

CONTEXTS AND AUDIENCES

Ezra-Nehemiah was probably written about 400 BCE. The early postexilic community in Jerusalem was small, only a fraction of the city's preexilic population. They left few archaeological remains and probably simply lived in repaired buildings left over from the preexilic period. We know from contemporary prophetic books that a spirit of frustrated expectations prevailed, at least at first. This attitude may be illustrated by the disappointment of those who could not rejoice over the commencement of work on the second temple because of their attachment to the first one (Ezra 3:12-13). The community's poverty, internal dissension, and inability to control its own destiny are demonstrated by the seventy years that lapsed between the completion of the temple (515 BCE) and the eventual reconstruction of the city wall (445). The Jewish community experienced constant hostility from its non-Jewish neighbors, especially those worshipers of Yahweh who lived to the north in the province of Samaria.

The community's division into parties and factions is evident from the various ideological positions represented in the restoration prophets (Haggai, Zechariah, Third Isaiah). There is evidence of a failed attempt to reinstitute some sort of Davidic rule centered on the figure of Zerubbabel (Hag 2:3-4). Economic tensions between a creditor class and a destitute debtor class are clearly reflected in Nehemiah 5. A gradual shift in language from Hebrew to Aramaic may have created further stresses on community solidarity. The scene depicted in Nehemiah 8:8 suggests a bilingual leadership class, but an Aramaic-speaking general populace.

To this harassed community living on the edge, Ezra-Nehemiah declares a word of legitimacy and divine election. You are the true Israel. Your temple worship is in direct continuity with everything Moses and David mandated. Do not despair over your powerless and enslaved political situation (described in Ezra 9:9 and Neh 9:36-37). Remember that the Persian kings have been used as instruments of God's plans for our community (Ezra 1:1-4; 6:22; 7:6, 27-28; Neh 1:11; 2:8). Do not be discouraged over the hostility of neighboring peoples or the ritually polluted state of so much that is around you (Ezra 9:11). Instead, rededicate yourself to adherence to the law of Moses in all areas of life—ritual, personal, and social. Confess your transgressions (Ezra 9:6-15; Neh 9:6-35) and commit yourselves to God's law (Neh 9:38–10:39). Carry on in the task of rebuilding the community, confident that you can count on God's help.

These powerful claims and challenges are advanced by the use of authoritative official documents, impressive lists, and vivid eyewitness narratives. The book seeks to make direct contact with its first readers by citing their own genealogies, in one case reaching down almost to their present moment (Neh 12:26). A series of strong imperatives are addressed to the readers to comfort them and rouse them to faith, action, and worship:

• "Let the house of God be rebuilt" (Ezra 5:15).
• "Make confession to the LORD . . . and do his will; separate yourselves from the peoples" (Ezra 10:11).
• "Come, let us rebuild the wall of Jerusalem" (Neh 2:17).
• "Do not be afraid of them. Remember the LORD . . . and fight" (Neh 4:14).
• "Eat the fat and drink sweet wine . . . and do not be grieved, for the joy of the LORD is your strength" (Neh 8:10).
• "Stand up and bless the LORD your God" (Neh 9:5).

THEMES

Legitimacy

Ezra-Nehemiah seeks to assure its readers that their temple community is legitimate and enjoys unbroken continuity with preexilic Israel. Those who return in Ezra 2 are the true Israel (v. 2*b*), in contrast to those others in Palestine who worship Yahweh (Ezra 4:2, 10). Only those who can prove their ancestry may serve as priests (2:62-63). The sites of the new altar and temple are explicitly identified as the original locations (2:68; 3:3; 5:15; 6:7). The original temple vessels carried off by the Babylonians are returned for use in the rebuilt shrine (1:7-11; 5:14-15; 6:5).[8] All ceremonies are performed correctly and according to scriptural prescriptions (Ezra 3:2, 4-5; 6:16-22; Neh 8:14, 18) and the arrangements of David and Solomon (Ezra 3:10-11; Neh 12:44-47). Even though the reconstruction of the temple and its community took place at the instigation of the Persian kings, it was really God who launched each of those royal actions (Ezra 1:1; 7:6, 27-28; Neh 1:11; 2:8).

The Law of God

The ideal community advocated by Ezra-Nehemiah reveres its scriptures. It centers its life on the law book of which Ezra was a scribe (Ezra 7:6, 12, 21) and that provided the grounds for his reforms. This book records the law of Moses (Ezra 7:6; Neh 8:1; 13:1). Because Ezra's reforms appear to allude to laws found in both Deuteronomy and Leviticus (Ezra 9:2 and Neh 8:14-15), Ezra's law book was probably something very close to the present form of the Pentateuch. The restored Jewish community lives and thrives because God's law revealed to Moses has been restored to it (Neh 8:1).[9]

Community Purity

Ezra-Nehemiah is concerned to preserve community purity. Those who faithfully keep the law and worship at the temple are to remain apart from other groups (Ezra 4:1-3; 10:11; Neh 2:20; 9:2; 10:28; 13:3). They are to avoid and even dissolve mixed marriages (Ezra 9–10; Neh 10:30; 13:23-29). The impure elements of the population, from whom the community must remain separate, are termed "the people(s) of the land." These ritually impure outsiders are hostile to the plans of the Jews (Ezra 3:3; 4:4), pollute themselves with the abominations of the Canaanites (Ezra 9:1-2), and fail to observe the sabbath (Neh 10:31). The exclusive circle of those considered to be the true people of God consists primarily of those who returned from Babylon, but it also includes others who are willing to remain aloof from those who practice impurity (Ezra 6:21).

Modern readers are likely to find that their own core values of universal human kinship are in sharp contrast to the exclusivist point of view advocated by Ezra-Nehemiah. However, it must be understood that biblical law demanded ritual purity as a requirement for communion with God, shared table fellowship, and participation in the sacrificial liturgy. Moreover, marriage in the ancient world inevitably involved extensive social and religious contact between the partners' two families. We should remember that beleaguered minority peoples have often felt it necessary to preserve their identity and culture by cutting themselves off from others.

NOTES

1. WHAT ARE WE READING?

1. The division of Samuel and Kings into two books developed from the practice of the Christian Greek Old Testament and surfaced in the Jewish Hebrew tradition only in the fifteenth century.

2. The Former Prophets along with the Latter Prophets (the major and minor prophets) make up the Prophets, the second of three divisions of the Hebrew canon. The separation of the Prophets into two subdivisions goes back to the early medieval period.

3. The canonical tradition of the Hebrew Bible considers both 1 and 2 Chronicles and Ezra-Nehemiah as single books. The Greek Old Testament tradition treated 1 and 2 Chronicles as separate books and sometimes divided Ezra-Nehemiah as well.

4. Supreme Court Justice Potter Stewart in 1964: "I shall not today attempt further to define [obscenity,] but I know it when I see it."

5. For a sobering popular account of this phenomenon, see James Loewen, *Lies My Teacher Told Me* (New York: New Press, 1995).

6. The classic example is Arnold Toynbee, *A Study of History* (New York: Oxford University Press, 1948–61).

7. The Moabite Stone, in *Ancient Near Eastern Texts Relating to the Old Testament,* ed. James Pritchard (Princeton: Princeton University Press, 1969), 320.

8. Burke Long, *1 Kings* The Forms of Old Testament Literature IX (Grand Rapids: Eerdmans, 1984), 250-51.

9. J. Huizinga, "A Definition of the Concept of History," in *Philosophy and History,* ed. R. Klibansky and H. Paton (Oxford: Clarendon, 1936), 9.

10. *Peloponnesian War* Loeb Classical Library (Cambridge: Harvard, 1928), I, xxii, 4.

11. Two opposing discussions of the relationship between history and biblical historiography are John Van Seters, *In Search of History* (New Haven: Yale University Press, 1983), 1-54, 209-48; and Baruch Halpern, *The First Historians* (San Francisco: Harper & Row, 1988), pp. 3-32.

2. THE HISTORICAL CONTEXT

1. For easily accessible reviews of the archaeological evidence for the entire preexilic period, see William Dever, *Recent Archaeological Discoveries and Biblical Research* (Seattle: University of Washington, 1990), and Amihai Mazar, *Archaeology and the Land of the Bible 10,000–586 B.C.E.* (New York: Doubleday, 1990), 232-549.

2. See Frank Frick, *The Formation of the State in Ancient Israel* (Sheffield: Almond, 1985).

3. The most important extrabiblical sources are readily available in *Ancient Near Eastern Texts Relating to the Old Testament,* ed. James Pritchard (Princeton: Princeton University Press, 1969). These include the Mesha Inscription (Moab, pp. 320-21), the Monolith Inscription of Shalmaneser III (Assyria, pp. 278-79), the Black Obelisk of Shalmaneser III (Assyria, p. 281), the Annals of Sennacherib (Assyria, pp. 287-88), the Siloam Inscription (Jerusalem, p. 321), the Babylonian Chronicle (esp. p. 564), and the Lachish Letters (Judah, pp. 321-22).

3. PATTERNS OF READING

1. For explanations and illustrations of the various methods of biblical interpretation, see John Barton, *Reading the Old Testament: Method in Bible Study* rev. ed. (Louisville: Westminster John Knox Press, 1997), and John Hayes and Carl Holladay, *Biblical Exegesis: A Beginner's Handbook* rev. ed. (Atlanta: John Knox Press, 1987). For a more technical approach, consult Odil Steck, *Old Testament Exegesis: A Guide to the Methodology* (Atlanta: Scholars Press, 1995).

2. A helpful and readable introduction to the interpretation of Old Testament narratives is Robert Alter, *The Art of Biblical Narrative* (New York: Basic Books, 1981). See also J. Cheryl Exum and David Clines, *The New Literary Criticism and the Hebrew Bible* (Sheffield: JSOT Press, 1993), and David Gunn and Danna Fewell, *Narrative in the Hebrew Bible* (Oxford: Oxford University Press, 1993).

3. The verb in Hebrew implies shortsighted and disbelieving behavior with a negative outcome that should have been foreseen.

4. Exaggeration is a common literary strategy. Men of military age numbering 1,300,000 would point to a total population of about 5 million. However, the total population of Palestine including the Trans-Jordan in the 1930s was only 1.5 million.

5. The disturbing "seven" in the Hebrew text of v. 13 (NRSV note) probably derives from the duration of the Egyptian famine (see Gen 41:30). The numerous textual notes in the NRSV indicate that the Hebrew text of this narrative was corrupted through successive acts of copying and has been restored from other textual traditions.

6. Hebrew has both a singular and plural "you."

7. The original boundary description moved from south to north to demarcate territory east of the Jordan and then went east to west across Israel's northernmost border. It ended with an indication of the south

border. The original boundary list can be reconstructed as follows: "From Aroer and from the city that is in the middle of the valley [Josh 13:9], Gad, and to Jazer . . . toward Gilead, and to the land under Hermon [conjecture; Josh 11:3] . . . toward Dan, 'Jaan' [Ain? Iyyon?], and around to Sidon . . . Fortress of Tyre [Josh 19:29], and all the cities of the Hivites and Canaanites . . . to the Negeb of Judah, Beer-sheba." The telegraphic style and wide spacing of the border points indicate that this was not a practical administrative document but a mental map intended to describe and claim Israel's territory.

8. However, not every difference is a matter of redaction. The text of Samuel used by the Chronicler was not the same as the one that has come down to us in the Hebrew text tradition. Chronicles frequently corresponds to textual readings of Samuel found in the Greek Old Testament and in the Dead Sea Scrolls. For example, the description of the angel in 1 Chronicles 21:16 reproduces a reading of 2 Samuel 24 preserved in one of the Dead Sea Scrolls.

9. For these proposals, see P. Kyle McCarter, *II Samuel* AB 9 (Garden City, N.Y.: Doubleday, 1984), 514-18.

4. DEUTERONOMISTIC HISTORY AND CHRONISTIC BOOKS

1. The classic description of DH is that of Martin Noth, *The Deuteronomistic History* (Sheffield: JSOT Press, 1981). See also Terence Fretheim, *Deuteronomic History* (Nashville: Abingdon Press, 1983), and Steven McKenzie, "Deuteronomistic History," in *Anchor Bible Dictionary* (New York: Doubleday, 1992), vol. 2, pp. 160-68, with the bibliography cited there.

2. Supplements were later added to the historian's core work. Thus Joshua 13–22, 24; Judges 1, 17–21; and 2 Samuel 21–24 are usually not considered to be part of the Deuteronomistic History. The placement of these expansions suggests that they were added after DH had been divided into individual books.

3. See also 1 Kgs 2:4; 8:20; 9:5; 11:13, 32; 2 Kgs 19:34; 20:6.

4. Some scholars have suggested that the presence of these prophetic narratives indicates that DH used an earlier written "prophetic history" or "prophetic record" as a basis for the early monarchy period. See Anthony Campbell, *Of Prophets and Kings* (Washington: Catholic Biblical Association, 1986).

5. The other chronological notices are Judg 4:3; 5:31; 6:1; 8:28; 9:22; 10:2-3, 8; 12:7, 9, 11, 14; 13:1. Samson's 20 years (Judg 15:20; 16:31) are included in the 40 years of 13:1, as is the 20-year captivity of the ark (1 Sam 7:2). The 40-year period of Eli (1 Sam 24:18) remains a disturbing factor and falls outside the system.

6. John Van Seters, *In Search of History* (New Haven: Yale University Press, 1983), 67.

7. The later, pessimistic version of DH further sharpened the attack against both Israel and Judah for worshiping "other gods" and venerating the host of heaven: 2 Kgs 17:7, 16-20.

8. The classic study is that of M. Noth, *The Chronicler's History* (Sheffield: JSOT Press, 1987).

5. THE BOOK OF JOSHUA

1. Richard Nelson, "Josiah in the Book of Joshua," *JBL* 100 (1981): 531-40.

2. Walter Brueggemann, *The Land: Place as Gift, Promise, and Challenge in Biblical Faith* (Philadelphia: Fortress Press, 1977); Norman Habel, *The Land Is Mine* (Minneapolis: Fortress Press, 1995).

3. The Mesha Inscription is an example of divine warrior theology used to glorify the Moabite god Chemosh; *ANET,* 320-21.

6. THE BOOK OF JUDGES

1. Ehud: 3:12, 15, and 30. Deborah: 4:1-3 and 4:23 plus 5:31. Gideon: 6:1, 6, and 8:28. Jephthah: 10:6-7, 10, and 11:33.

2. The contribution of DH is usually recognized most clearly in 2:6–3:6; 3:7-11 (Othniel); 3:12, 14-15, 30; 4:1-3, 23; 5:31; 6:1, 6-10; 8:28, 33-35; 10:6-16; 11:33; 13:1.

3. For a provocative reading of Judges based on the politics of gender violence, see Mieke Bal, *Death and Dissymmetry* (Chicago: University of Chicago Press, 1988). Several scholars approach Judges from a variety of interpretive perspectives in *Judges and Method,* ed. Gale A. Yee (Minneapolis: Fortress Press, 1995).

4. There are other differences in perspective between the two books. Judah's capture of Hebron (Judg 1:10) is credited to Caleb in Joshua 15:14 and Judges 1:20. Deborah's adversary Jabin is also named as king of Hazor a generation earlier in Joshua 11:1-11, a text which reports Hazor's complete destruction.

5. Lawrence Stager, "The Archaeology of the Family in Ancient Israel," BASOR 206 (1985): 1-35.

6. This literary analysis depends in part on Barry Webb, *The Book of the Judges: An Integrated Reading* (Sheffield: JSOT Press, 1987).

7. For a reading that understands Judges to be pervaded by irony, see Lillian Klein, *The Triumph of Irony in the Book of Judges* (Sheffield: Almond, 1988).

8. Important studies of Judges from a feminist perspective are Athalya Brenner, *A Feminist Companion to Judges* (Sheffield: JSOT Press, 1993); Mieke Bal, *Murder and Difference: Gender, Genre, and Scholarship in Sisera's Death* (Bloomington: Indiana University, 1988); and Michael O'Connor, "The Women in the Book of Judges," HAR 10 (1986): 277-93.

9. A fable is an illustrative story in which animals or plants have speaking parts.

10. The name *Hormah* in Judges 1:17 is a wordplay on the Hebrew word *herem,* the holy war ban inflicted when the city was devoted to destruction.

7. THE BOOKS OF 1 AND 2 SAMUEL

1. See Patrick Miller and J. Roberts, *The Hand of the Lord: A Reassessment of the "Ark Narrative" of 1 Samuel* (Baltimore: Johns Hopkins University Press, 1977). For the political purposes of the Ark Story, see A. Alström, "The Travels of the Ark: A Religio-Political Composition," *JNES* 43 (1984): 141-49. The classic 1926 study of this and the Throne Succession Story is available in English as Leonhard Rost, *The Succession to the Throne of David* (Sheffield: Almond, 1982), 6-34 (Ark Story), and 65-114 (Throne Succession).

2. For literary issues, see James Ackerman, "Knowing Good and Evil: A Literary Analysis of the Court History in 2 Samuel 9–20 and 1 Kings 1–2," *JBL* 109 (1990): 41-60; and Gerhard von Rad, "The Beginnings of Historical Writing in Ancient Israel," in *The Problem of the Hexateuch and Other Essays* (London: Oliver & Boyd, 1966), 166-204.

3. Perhaps Samuel's role as counterpart to Saul is signaled by the wordplay on his name offered by 1 Samuel 1:20 (a pun on "asked"), which would fit Saul's name much better.

4. A text of Samuel found among the Dead Sea Scrolls revealed a previously lost paragraph that originally began the story of Saul's first victory. The NRSV prints this between 1 Samuel 10:27 and 11:1.

5. The Old Testament also preserves 2 Samuel 22 as Psalm 18.

6. For a reading of Samuel that takes its political dimensions seriously, see Walter Brueggemann, *First and Second Samuel* (Louisville: John Knox, 1990).

8. THE BOOKS OF 1 AND 2 KINGS

1. These framing notices are fragmentary until Rehoboam receives the full form (1 Kgs 14:21-22, 29-31). Concluding statements are missing for certain kings, for example the victims of Jehu's purge. Jehu lacks an introductory formula because of the unusual circumstances of his accession. Joash of Israel is inexplicably provided with two closing formulas (2 Kgs 13:12-13; 14:15-16).

2. For a connected literary and theological reading of Kings, see Richard Nelson, *First and Second Kings* (Atlanta: John Knox, 1987).

3. Richard Nelson, "God and the Heroic Prophet: Preaching the Stories of Elijah and Elisha," *Quarterly Review* 9 (Summer 1989): 93-105.

4. Compare the unrealized offers of the throne of Israel made to Solomon and Jeroboam in 1 Kgs 2:4; 8:25; 9:5; 11:37-38.

5. The reign of Jehu closes in 2 Kgs 10:36, but that of Joash of Judah does not formally commence until 12:1.

6. Richard Nelson, "The Altar of Ahaz: A Revisionist View," HAR 10 (1986): 267-75.

7. The text provides no context or motivation for Neco's deed. Had the author wished to describe a battle (as is often assumed), this could certainly have been stated more clearly. See Richard Nelson, "Realpolitik in Judah (687–609 B.C.E.)," in *Scripture and Context II* (Winona Lake, Ind.: Eisenbrauns, 1983), 177-89.

8. Other scholars propose an exilic work subsequently overlaid by two redactions oriented toward prophecy and law respectively. Still other proposals suggest that the history originally ended with the reign of Hezekiah (see 2 Kgs 18:5) or that a preexilic prophetic history served as the original basis for the work.

9. THE BOOKS OF 1 AND 2 CHRONICLES

1. A handy tool for this is James Newsome, *A Synoptic Harmony of Samuel, Kings, and Chronicles* (Grand Rapids: Baker Book House, 1986).
2. Unlike the situation in Kings, "throne of Israel" in Chronicles refers to reign over the whole nation.
3. On the theology and role of the priests in Chronicles, see Richard Nelson, *Raising Up A Faithful Priest* (Louisville: Westminster John Knox, 1993), 130-40.

10. THE BOOKS OF EZRA AND NEHEMIAH

1. Shemaryahu Talmon, "Ezra and Nehemiah," in *The Literary Guide to the Bible* (Cambridge: Harvard University Press, 1987), 357-64.
2. The Persian kings mentioned in Ezra-Nehemiah are Cyrus (559–530 BCE), Darius I (522–486), Ahasuerus (Xerxes, 486–465), and Artaxerxes I (465–424).
3. It is possible that Ezra was appointed in 398, the seventh year of Artaxerxes II rather than of Artaxerxes I (Ezra 7:1, 8). If this is the case, then Ezra would have worked a generation *after* Nehemiah. Adopting this conclusion would mean that the author made a glaring historical mistake about relatively recent events. Such a blunder seems unlikely and would hardly have been accepted by the original readership.
4. According to this view, the seventh month referred to in Nehemiah 7:73*b* and 8:2 would have directly followed the fifth month of Year 7 of Artaxerxes, when Ezra first arrived in Jerusalem (Ezra 7:8-9).
5. The common interpretation is that those who remembered the first temple were disappointed at the size or inferior quality of the second's foundation. The NRSV translation of Ezra 3:12 implies this. More probably, they were dissatisfied simply because it was not the same temple that they had cherished. My translation would be: "Old people who had seen the former house on its foundation (this was *the* house in their eyes) were weeping."
6. The Hebrew text here is obscure: "and there were from them (among them?) wives and they set sons." The NRSV restores the text from a Greek translation, 1 Esdras 9:36.
7. There is no reason to take Nehemiah 9:6 as a prayer of Ezra as the NRSV does; see the NRSV text note.
8. Peter Ackroyd, "The Temple Vessels—A Continuity Theme," in *Studies in the Religion of Ancient Israel* VTSup 23 (Leiden: Brill, 1972), 166-81.
9. Dennis McCarthy, "Covenant and Law in Chronicles-Nehemiah," *CBQ* 44 (1982): 25-44.

Selected Bibliography

Ackroyd, Peter. *The Chronicler and His Age*. Sheffield: JSOT, 1991.

Alter, Robert. *The Art of Biblical Narrative*. New York: Basic Books, 1981.

Alter, Robert, and Frank Kermode, eds. *The Literary Guide to the Bible*. Cambridge: Belknap, 1987.

Bal, Mieke. *Death and Dissymmetry: The Politics of Coherence in Judges*. Chicago: University of Chicago, 1988.

———. *Murder and Difference: Gender, Genre, and Scholarship in Sisera's Death*. Bloomington: Indiana University, 1988.

Bar-Efrat. *Narrative Art in the Bible*. Sheffield: JSOT, 1989.

Barton, John. *Reading the Old Testament*. Rev. ed. Louisville: Westminster John Knox Press, 1997.

Brenner, Athalya, ed. *A Feminist Companion to Judges*. Sheffield: Sheffield Academic Press, 1993.

———, ed. *A Feminist Companion to Samuel and Kings*. Sheffield: Sheffield Academic Press, 1994.

Brueggemann, Walter. *David's Truth in Israel's Imagination and Memory*. Philadelphia: Westminster, 1985.

———. *First and Second Samuel*. Louisville: John Knox, 1990.

Doorly, William. *Obsession with Justice: The Story of the Deuteronomists*. New York: Paulist Press, 1994.

Duke, Rodney. *The Persuasive Appeal of the Chronicler: A Rhetorical Analysis*. Sheffield: Almond, 1990.

Eskenazi, Tamara. *In an Age of Prose: A Literary Approach to Ezra-Nehemiah.* Atlanta: Scholars Press, 1988.

Eslinger, Lyle. *Into the Hands of the Living God.* Sheffield: Almond, 1989.

———. *The Kingship of God in Crisis: A Close Reading of 1 Samuel 1–12.* Sheffield: Almond, 1985.

Exum, J. Cheryl, and David Clines. *The New Literary Criticism and the Hebrew Bible.* Sheffield: JSOT Press, 1993.

Fokkelman, Jan. *Narrative Art and Poetry in the Books of Samuel.* 2 vols. Assen: Van Gorcum, 1981, 1986.

Fretheim, Terence. *Deuteronomic History.* Nashville: Abingdon Press, 1983.

Gunn, David. *The Fate of King Saul: An Interpretation of a Biblical Story.* Sheffield: University of Sheffield, 1980.

———. *The Story of King David.* Sheffield: University of Sheffield, 1978.

Gunn, David, and Diana Fewell. *Narrative in the Hebrew Bible.* Oxford: Oxford University Press, 1993.

Halpern, Baruch. *The First Historians: The Hebrew Bible and History.* San Francisco: Harper & Row, 1988.

Hawk, Daniel. *Every Promise Fulfilled: Contesting Plots in Joshua.* Louisville: Westminster John Knox Press, 1991.

Hayes, John, and Carl Holladay. *Biblical Exegesis: A Beginner's Handbook.* Rev. ed. Atlanta: John Knox Press, 1987.

Kelley, Brian. *Retribution and Eschatology in Chronicles.* Sheffield: Sheffield Academic Press, 1996.

Klein, Lillian. *The Triumph of Irony in the Book of Judges.* Sheffield: Almond, 1988.

McKenzie, Steven, and Steven Haynes. *To Each Its Own Meaning: An Introduction to Biblical Criticisms and Their Applications.* Louisville: Westminster John Knox Press, 1993.

McKnight, Edgar. *The Bible and the Reader: An Introduction to Literary Criticism.* Philadelphia: Westminster, 1985.

Miller, Patrick, and J. Roberts. *The Hand of the Lord: A*

Reassessment of the "Ark Narrative" of 1 Samuel. Baltimore: Johns Hopkins University Press, 1977.

Miscall, Peter. *1 Samuel: A Literary Reading*. Bloomington: Indiana University, 1986.

Mitchell, Gordon. *Together in the Land*. Sheffield: JSOT, 1993.

Mullen, Edward. *Narrative History and Ethnic Boundaries: The Deuteronomistic History and the Creation of Israelite National Identity*. Atlanta: Scholars Press, 1993.

Nelson, Richard. *First and Second Kings*. Atlanta: John Knox, 1987.

———. *Raising Up a Faithful Priest: Community and Priesthood in Biblical Theology*. Louisville: Westminster John Knox Press, 1993.

Noll, Kurt. *The Faces of David*. Sheffield: Sheffield Academic Press, 1997.

Noth, Martin. *The Chronicler's History*. Sheffield: JSOT, 1987.

———. *The Deuteronomistic History*. Sheffield: JSOT, 1981.

Polzin, Robert. *Moses and the Deuteronomist*. New York: Seabury Press, 1980.

———. *Samuel and the Deuteronomist*. San Francisco: Harper & Row, 1989.

Rost, Leonhard. *The Succession to the Throne of David*. Sheffield: Almond, 1982.

Rowlett, Lori. *Joshua and the Rhetoric of Violence*. Sheffield: Sheffield Academic Press, 1996.

Steck, Otto. *Old Testament Exegesis: A Guide to the Methodology*. Atlanta: Scholars Press, 1995.

Sternberg, Meir. *The Poetics of Biblical Narrative*. Bloomington: Indiana University Press, 1985.

Throntveit, Mark. *Ezra-Nehemiah*. Louisville: John Knox, 1992.

Van Seters, John. *In Search of History*. New Haven: Yale, 1983.

Walsh, Jerome. *1 Kings*. Collegeville, Minn.: Liturgical Press, 1996.

Webb, Barry. *The Book of Judges: An Integrated Reading.* Sheffield: JSOT, 1987.

Yee, Gail, ed. *Judges and Method: New Approaches in Biblical Studies.* Minneapolis: Fortress Press, 1995.

Index

187

INDEX

INDEX